Peg Leg Pete

Peg Leg Pete

by
MEL
ELLIS

HOLT, RINEHART AND WINSTON
New York   Chicago   San Francisco

For Sibyll Yug, Roy Lekfield
and in memory of Jerome Washicheck, Sr.

Peg Leg Pete's Special Friends

Published simultaneously in Canada by Holt, Rinehart
and Winston of Canada, Limited.
Library of Congress Catalog Number: 72–78130
Published, January, 1973
Second Printing, February, 1973
ISBN: 0–03–001366–6
Printed in the United States of America

Apologia

Dear Mary, Dianne, and Deborah:

Some of the incidents in this book, as you will discover upon reading it, are made from the magic of imagination because there was no certain way to ascertain the facts.

But you will also know, looking back on the life and times of Peg Leg Pete, that basically the truth about this unconquerable mallard drake has been little altered or much exaggerated.

I'm sure sometimes I've misquoted each of you, perhaps even put words in your mouth. But that is sometimes the way it is with me and my memory.

Yet it seems, and I hope it is true, that whatever has served to poignantly make a point has not been lost in the spidery web of time. But, if an apology is in order, you have it, and if I took what you might construe as liberties with a few of the lesser facts, I hope you will agree that the real, the greater truth has been served.

Yours with love,
Dad

(1

It was the thirteenth of December, the year nineteen hundred and sixty-six that Peg Leg Pete came into our lives. It was cold. During the night it had snowed. When I got up to turn up the thermostat it was still dark. I walked out onto the sun porch and looked down across our fifteen acres to where we've got four spring-fed, man-made ponds. I could see a beam of light shining through a latticed screen of bare willow branches, streaking like lightning flashes across the snow, hiding furtively behind stands of cattails. I knew one of my daughters was down there checking the traps which had been set for the muskrats which were making a sieve of the dike which held the water in the largest, the three-acre pond.

I walked through the house with its tiny night lights glowing softly from wall fixtures in each room and, standing in the living room, looked out the picture window. Through a thick stand of blue and Norway spruce I could detect another light. One of my other daughters was feeding the two horses and chopping ice for a hole in Fish Pond so they could drink.

I could hear the coffeepot beginning to bubble. I had turned it on when I went through the kitchen. I walked back through the house and in the dark kitchen the burner of the stove glowed a brilliant red. I took the pot from the heat and then turned on a light and poured a cup of coffee.

The girl who had been feeding the horses came in first. It was Debbie. Her cheeks were red, and she was blowing on her fingers.

"Much ice?" I asked.

"Not too much."

"What's keeping Dianne?" I asked. Debbie shrugged. Dianne was the girl checking the traps. She was twelve. Debbie was fifteen. Upstairs I could hear the eight-year-old girl stirring. They would all have to hurry if they were going to be on time for school.

"Want some coffee?" I asked Debbie.

"No. I'll take chocolate." She got out a saucepan and put some milk on the still-hot stove burner.

I heard Dianne's boots on the back steps and wondered why she hadn't gone in through the bottom basement door. Muddy boots weren't allowed in the house. Checking traps was a muddy job. So I knew something had gone wrong and got up in time to swing open the heavy door for her.

As if anticipating my question, she said, "It's a duck. In one of the muskrat traps." She held the duck in her arms. It was a mallard drake with a shimmering emerald head, a shining eye, and a banana-yellow bill. One leg hung limply by shreds. The other leg was braced against Dianne's gray checkered coat.

For a moment I was nonplused. It was too early. I hadn't had enough coffee. But the blood dripping from

2

the dangling leg moved me to say, "Well, bring him in."

She came in, out of the still-dark night, out of the cold. The mallard cringed, and then struck out at me with his bonehard bill. Through my light red robe I could feel it hit a rib.

"Well, he's tough, anyway," I said.

"But you're going to have to kill him?" Dianne made it a question. Debbie was leaning through the kitchen door to where we were standing on the sun porch.

"He's beautiful," she said. "He's too beautiful to kill."

"What is it?" Mary had come down. She was dressed for school. When she saw the injured mallard, she said, "Oh, Daddy!"

"Spread some newspaper on the kitchen table," I said, "and we'll have a look."

Debbie moved the cups and spread the papers. Dianne came in leaving muddy tracks behind. She handed me the drake. I could feel the power in his wings as he struggled to be free.

"Debbie, you'll have to hold him while I look," I handed her the drake.

The light above the kitchen table was on a pull-down cord. I lowered it so it focused on the patient much like a light in an operating room.

"Well, we've got to stop the bleeding. Get me a rubber band." I heard Dianne rummaging through the junk drawer. She handed me the rubber band.

"Hold him sideways, flat to the table," I said to Debbie.

"He's strong," she said.

"You're stronger."

She turned the drake so the mutilated leg was up and facing me. Carefully, I held the rubber band wide,

3

slipped it over the webs, up the bright orange leg as high as the drumstick, the thigh. Then gently I let go until it was snugged into place. The bleeding stopped.

I was about to take the dangling leg between my fingers, when I heard Gwen, my wife's voice, right behind me, "What's going on out here?" She was in a long, bright green, granny gown.

"It's a duck," Mary said.

"Caught in a muskrat trap," Dianne added.

It was enough of an explanation for anyone who lived at our house. My wife leaned over between the children to see. For an instant I thought I saw a trace of nausea pinch her face.

Being squeamish, however, is not one of her weaknesses. The Victorian prerogative of women to faint at the sight of blood would make life difficult for any living at Little Lakes—the name we had given our fifteen acres.

In fact, all five of my daughters (two, SuZanne and Sharon, had gone off to be married by the time Peg Leg Pete came along), and both of my wives (one, Bernice, had died), could pluck a bat from the bedroom drapes and ease it out the window, or pick up a mouse (dead or alive) . . . or mend a head.

"What are you going to do with him?" my wife, Gwen, asked.

I lifted the leg. Only white threads, tendons, held it in place. "Well, you know what would be best," I answered her.

Everybody knew what I meant, but Mary was the first to respond, "Just don't expect me to eat him. I couldn't! I wouldn't! And, I won't!"

I knew without asking that Mary's sentiments were,

4

of course, held by all the others. It was one of the reasons why long ago I'd given up trying to raise ducks, chickens, squabs, or pheasants for the table. They sometimes even became attached to certain trout in Clear Pool, especially if a fish had a physical deformity which set it apart when they all swarmed to the surface to snatch at the floating pellets of food. Then if one of their fish friends happened to be caught while angling for a meal, back it went. That's why, under our acres are probably buried enough rabbits alone to feed a family for a long time.

To me, of course, it was a waste. I came from a father who had been a trapper, part-time market hunter, and as a boy it had been part of my job to keep the larder well supplied with fish and game. I accomplished my job with zeal, almost a vengeance, and went on to become outdoor editor of a metropolitan newspaper, the *Milwaukee Journal,* and associate editor of a national hunting and fishing magazine, *Field and Stream.* During the course of these journalistic duties I, of course, killed more than a score of deer, many moose, elk . . . not to mention coyotes, mountain lions, jaguars . . . and boatloads of ducks, and wagonloads of pheasants, quail, grouse, doves . . . almost every animal and bird which could legally be hunted on our two continents.

So mine, of course, was a somewhat jaundiced eye. But staring at me as I held the orange, webbed foot with its bright nails, were four pairs of eyes—two blue, one brown, and one gray-green—which almost seemed to dare me to put the axe to this mutilated mallard.

"Well, we'll see," I said. "First let's loosen the tourniquet to let a little blood down."

When a drop of blood appeared, I let the rubber band go tight again.

"Get me one of those wooden ice cream spoons," I said, referring to the kind attached to tiny cups of ice cream. Mary knew what I meant, and relieved, I suppose, darted off to get one.

I split the tiny wooden spoon, made two splints. I tried them on for size, held them to each side of the mangled leg, but it was hopeless. There just was nothing left to splint. The leg was dangling.

Finally I said, "The leg's got to go."

Maybe we'd known it all along. But cutting off a limb, even though it be on a bird or a beast, is something you think about twice, especially if you don't plan on eventually killing the patient.

"Get me your sharpest scissors," I said, turning to Gwen. She went to the bedroom and came back with her best.

"Tired, Debbie?" I asked. All along she'd been holding the drake. There were sweat beads on her upper lip. They shone in the bright light.

"I can hang on."

"Okay," and turning to Gwen, I said, "Get me the Bactine, some silk thread and some bandages from clean rags."

Everybody, except Debbie of course, bustled away to get something. She held the mallard, who by now had relaxed somewhat, and let his emerald head hang so the yellow bill was touching the newspapers on the table.

The things I had asked for arrived in quick succession. "Okay, now, hang on tight, Deb, because I'm going to cut the tendons. He might fight you."

Carefully I lifted the dangling leg until it was in its

6

natural position. The pair of sharp little scissors put out glints of silver as I spread the blades and positioned them. Then with a sharp snap I severed the tendons. I could see a tremor run through the drake. The foot was in my hand. Suddenly, for no good reason I could think of, I felt guilty and looked around at the others. They were looking at the foot too, so I put it down, laid it on the table, where it looked strangely like an orange peel, except once it moved, flexed a little.

Finally I took my eyes off the severed leg and foot and went back to work. I put rags beneath the stump and poured on Bactine. A few drops of blood appeared. I poured on a little more Bactine. The bleeding stopped. I tied the shredded tendon ends together with three wrap-arounds of silk thread. Then I poured on more Bactine.

"Now the bandages," I said. Gwen handed them to me. I took off the rubber tourniquet and wrapped until I had a huge ball of cloth around the stump. Then I put the rubber band over the lump of rags, leaned back and said, "That's all I can do."

Debbie's hands must have relaxed with my words, because all of a sudden the drake was free, and levering with his one good leg, bounced into the air and flew into the kitchen wall to drop to the linoleum with a thud.

I was on him before he could try it again. "A cardboard box," I said. "A deep one with a good top so we can keep him in the dark."

The box came out of the basement. The drake went into it. The cover was closed. There was a moment of scrambling in the box, then silence except for the ticking of the clock on the wall behind us.

I turned to look at the clock. It was long past time for the children to get to school on time.

I went over to the sink to wash my hands. Gwen began picking up, cleaning the table. Debbie carried the cardboard box carefully to where the December sun now slanted through the wide windows of the sun porch.

"What'll I do with the leg?" Gwen asked.

"Throw it in the garbage."

Behind me everyone went suddenly silent. I turned. They were all staring at me. "All right then," I said, "Mary see if you can find a place to get through the frost line. Then bury it." I turned back to the sink to finish washing my hands. Above the splashing of water in the sink I said, "Just because you got out of school this morning don't think you're going to make a day of it. This afternoon you all go to school."

(2

If my family's feelings about ducks might perhaps have somewhat anthropomorphic overtones, be assured, if I have come to admire and be amazed by ducks—particularly mallards—in the beginning I had no illusions about, for instance, their practicality.

In the beginning a duck was something to shoot or butcher and then eat, or if permitted to live, then to be raised as a Mata Hari to attract other ducks to the gun.

My earliest recollection of ducks goes back to about 1917, or even earlier, when I was about four or five, and my father raised them to be used as live decoys to entice others, the wild ones, within range of his Remington.

I remember one little brown hen in particular, because she insisted on nesting beneath the front porch steps of our house in Juneau, Wisconsin. The house still stands (I saw it the other day), and from the outside it looks remarkably as I remember it, but the outhouse is, of course, gone, as is the shed for wood (we burned wood for heat) in which my father also housed his live decoys.

Most vividly I remember the mallard under the front porch leaving the nest one early summer with a file of bronze and buff babies in tow—though one egg remained on the nest.

I can remember my father saying, "We'll have to see if it was fertile or not." He took the egg around back of the woodshed and broke it on a stone.

Then, there lay a duckling, wet and somewhat bloodied, but still struggling for life. The sight of the helpless, injured bit of life amidst the wreckage of its own olive eggshells made such an imprint on my mind that today, more than fifty years later, I can see its tiny, open eyes, its delicate webbed feet, its down, wet with egg white plastered to its body.

I don't think it occurred to me that the duckling might be rescued, be saved, kept alive. I'm sure I only waited to see what my father's decision would be, and when he lifted a piece of cordwood and mashed the duckling to a pulp, though I may have been momentarily horrified, I accepted it as the proper thing to do.

My father was not a cruel man, only practical. At the time he was just starting an automobile agency and studying nights to make up for his lack of formal education. My mother was sick and in bed much of the time, and a brother of hers, still in high school, was our "hired girl." There already were three children, of whom I was the oldest, so who had time to nurse a duckling back from the edge of death?

Nevertheless, the sight of the piece of cordwood coming down on the helpless embryo never left me. At many and often odd times all through the years it has suddenly popped into my mind—vivid as the day it happened—so I suppose, in some strange way, it must have affected me deeply.

One thing it didn't do, however, was make me squeamish about killing ducks, because as soon as I was twelve I had my own .410-gauge shotgun, and if at first I rarely leveled it on waterfowl, I was a scourge so far as rabbits and squirrels were concerned.

What's more, I started raising my own live decoys—mallards, bought at fifty cents, and sometimes a black and white English caller, purchased for three dollars, to breed voice and svelte bodies into stock which sometimes had grown outsized from intermingling with tame, barnyard stock.

It was the custom then, when live decoys were still legal, to mate ducks selectively for size (small so they could be carried in cages in tiny duck skiffs), and for voice (so a wild flock on the horizon could hear them).

Most of the ducks I then raised have, over the years, become anonymous. But there was one, Lily, who not only turned out to be a deadly Mata Hari of the marshes, but such an individual in her own right, that today, if I support any of the anthropomorphic sentiments of my wife and children, surely she must get her share of the credit, or as some might say, blame.

Lily was always a free soul. Only once did I shackle her, and that was enough. She didn't fight the rubber-covered wire ring around her neck, or the tether fastened to a tiny anchor on the bottom of the river. She just sulked, never once opened her mouth, even when the feeding call was sounded, even when I took the drake and hid him back of where my boat had been shoved into the rushes.

11

Never after, though she worked several seasons before she disappeared, and before the United States Fish and Wildlife Service (now Bureau of Sport Fisheries and Wildlife) outlawed live decoys, did she feel any restraint.

What's more, while all my other decoys avoided me and had to be caught each time there was a training session at the end of a leash, Lily would sit on the bank of the river preening and calmly permit me to pick her up.

During those days, we moved our decoys out to Rock River in fall. Here we kept them in huge wire pens partly in and partly out of the water so their bodies became accustomed to continual wetting and their oil glands functioned smoothly enough to keep them from becoming sinkers.

When I was at school, hunters who lived at the river fed the ducks. But Lily could not abide the cage, so we let her free and she always stayed close, and if I was visiting she took to following me into our river cottage where she'd promptly wing to a tabletop for bread and milk, which she much preferred to our ducks' regular ration of corn.

The first time I took Lily on an actual hunt, we left about an hour before sunset. It was an opening day, and it was my intention to sleep in the hay in the bottom of my boat so no one would preempt my right to my blind. Since I was afraid of losing her in strange waters, I put her in a cage similar to those in which nestled three other hens and a drake.

Lily looked disconsolate, sitting humped up and with her wings drooping. So after rowing about a quarter mile, I took her out and lifted her to the skiff's bow. She stood there then, like a figurehead, head high, eyes bright, looking, looking.

On the way to the blind it got dark. After I shoved in where I had built my hiding place of cattails, I turned the flashlight to the bow of the boat. There she was, perched on one leg, her bill and part of her head beneath a wing—sound asleep.

In the morning, about an hour before dawn, while I was putting out the wooden decoys, she jumped overboard, had a drink, and then jumped back in to nestle down in the hay. Later, when it was near dawn and almost shooting time, I anchored the other three hens out near the wooden flotilla, and then hid the drake back in the reeds.

When I poled my skiff back into its hideaway, Lily jumped over the side and swimming out, took her position with the other hens. Behind me then, the confused drake quacked quietly. Out front Lily's three sisters of intrigue screamed at the top of their voices. Then, from far and near, came answering quacks of wild ducks and decoys. Lily never opened her bill. Instead she dipped for an occasional tendril or scooped up a throatful of duck wort. Sometimes she stretched her wings in a water-shivering duck yawn and swam about as though examining the area I had selected to hunt.

It was nearly shooting time when I saw her lift her head, as though listening and looking. Finally she quacked tentatively, waited and then sang out. Within seconds I heard the flock swish over and then saw them make their turn. Before the echo of Lily's invitation had died, they were dropping with set wings into the open water of the V I had left between the wooden decoys, and so the shooting started.

13

When it was over, and the sun was warm above, I picked up. All the way home my duck Delilah preened from her vantage point forward in the boat. When the bow ground onto homeshore gravel, she hopped down, waddled over to the pens where scores of ducks were imprisoned, and after a little headbobbing "hello" walked to the house.

She sat on the stoop waiting while I carried her fellow Fifth Columnists to the decoy pen and straightened out the anchor strings on the wooden ones so they'd be ready for the next day. When I came up and went through the kitchen door she followed and flew up onto the table for her luncheon of bread and milk.

Lily's only fault, if it was a fault, was that she considered herself folks. I doubt that it ever occurred to her that she might be a duck. Probably a look into a mirror would have astonished her, if, of course, she would ever have recognized the image as her own.

I do not make these observations lightly. I have seen other ducks that thought they were people. More than once, my children have taken incubator-hatched ducklings as pets, and I'm sure these ducks grew up to think they were people.

Lily and I came to a parting of the ways under sad circumstances. It began one autumn day when an uncle of mine was training a young Labrador retriever. The trainee made the mistake of picking Lily up off the lawn. At this indignity she promptly rapped the rash pup over the eyes with her stout wings, and clamped onto his nose with her plierslike bill.

The dog was doomed. We knew at once it would never again approach anything which smelled like a duck. My uncle was furious. He insisted that she be penned. And so she was—for the first time since the day she first took corn from my hand.

Penned, perhaps Lily realized her true status. Next morning when I came to get her to go for a hunt all her self-assurance, her jauntiness, had evaporated. She looked like, well, merely like a duck. And when she took her place on the bow of the boat she slumped, let her wings droop.

I hunted an open-water blind that day on the big lake to the south. I put out the wooden decoys so the fast swinging diver ducks which worked bigger water would see their V. Then I put the live decoys close to shore. As was her custom, Lily hopped off the bow into the water, but instead of joining the other three hens she turned and swam away into the gray morning.

All day then I journeyed from one end of the lake to the other, sounding the feeding call and watching, asking questions of other hunters. When the sun set I knew Lily had left for good.

And now I thought about Lily, and I thought about the unborn duck being crushed, and I thought about all the other mallards down through the long but exciting years as I carried the box which held Peg Leg Pete to the quiet of the basement, to a place near the warmth of the furnace.

When the children came home from school that night they brought in corn from the pen where there were tame ducks, rabbits, pheasants, and one woodchuck (sleeping now, far below the frost line in a burrow he had dug). But the wild mallard refused the corn, though it hammered their hands, wrists, and arms with savage bill thrusts until there were red welts which would surely discolor and turn into black-and-blue bruises.

A larger box was brought in from the garage, and the mallard transferred. A pan of water was put down, another of corn, and the box was covered over with an old coat.

"Think he'll eat?" Mary asked, as we came upstairs.

"He'll eat," Debbie said, "when he gets hungry enough."

"Maybe not," Dianne said, and I suppose she was thinking of the injured hawk we had force fed by prying open its sharp, curved beak to push tiny pellets of hamburger down its throat.

"We'll just have to wait and see," I said. "No use worrying about it now."

Well, the mallard didn't eat, and if it drank water, it did so when no one was watching.

After two days, I said, "This will never do. He's starving to death."

Usually this amounted to an ultimatum, and the children knew it. There had been injured wild pheasants, songbirds, cottontails, squirrels . . . many species we'd tried to rescue from one mishap or another which wouldn't eat. When all our efforts at feeding them failed, rather than permit a slow, agonizing death by starvation, they had been killed. I, of course, was always the executioner, and no matter how much my children loved me, they eyed me strangely, if not with suspicion, for hours after the deed had been done and they had finished with the last rites.

"Maybe if we put him with the other ducks," Debbie suggested.

The "other" ducks were a white Rouen named Gertie, a Muscovy drake named Waddle, a Pekin hen named Greta, and two somewhat, but not quite, wild mallard drakes named Aristotle and Plato. They lived in winter in a sixteen- by sixteen-foot hut which had about three feet of leaves on a dirt floor.

The ducks were not permitted out of the hut in winter, because their feet were so vulnerable to the cold, and because the Muscovy drake's cherry-bright comb always froze, turned black and then dropped off.

"We could try," I said to Debbie, "but I think we'd better separate him from the other drakes. They might try to kill him."

So in a wire enclosure, of which we had many kinds of all shapes and sizes, the duck was carried out into the cold on Saturday.

17

The other ducks chose to ignore the intruder, and the wild one lay on his side staring through the wire at the strange assortment of cousins around him.

Then we put in corn, counting it—fifteen kernels. And we put in a deep dish of water.

Naturally, it being Saturday, the children wanted to stay and watch. "Best leave him alone now," I said.

That night when they fed the other ducks they counted the kernels of corn in the wild one's cage. There still were fifteen. The water had been spilled, so obviously the drake had been threshing about.

"He can't go for too long," Gwen said that night at the supper table.

"No he can't," I agreed, "especially not out there in the cold. Just keeping warm takes a lot of eating."

"Maybe we ought to bring him back in," Mary said.

"If worse comes to worst, I suppose we will have to," I said.

Suddenly Dianne pushed her chair back and got up from the table. Flicking on the sun room light she walked out of the kitchen.

I was on the verge of scolding her for so unceremoniously leaving the table in the middle of a meal without asking to be excused, when she said, "Do you know how cold it is out there?"

Nobody answered her. Coming back in after switching off the light, she said, "It's down to twenty." The thermometer was affixed to the house on the outside where it was visible through a sun-room window.

"Well, it's warmer in the duck pen," Debbie said.

"Not much," Dianne argued.

"Well, let's bring him in," Mary urged.

I put down my knife and fork and motioned for silence. "He won't freeze. Now he won't eat in the box in the basement, so we can at least give it a try out there."

Next morning was Sunday, and chores had to be done before church, but there was time to stay abed at least until daylight. But Mary didn't. She was outside with a flashlight before dawn, and then from our downstairs bedroom I could hear her excited voice upstairs, "There were only twelve kernels of corn! He must have eaten three!"

I knew it might be so, but I also knew that he might have scattered the kernels, and then they would be lost among the leaves if he'd done any bouncing around during the night.

My wife was coming awake and I said to her, "How do we keep getting into things like this? When I was a kid every crippled duck without gangrene went straight to the oven, and we were darned glad to get it."

Gwen yawned. "Maybe it's partly your fault."

"My fault?" I raised to an elbow in bed.

"Admit it. You're getting soft. You've been getting softer every year I've known you. The kids sense it."

Well, it was true, I suppose. Gradually, over a period of twenty years, I'd hunted less and less. Gradually, especially after encountering hordes of gunners on public hunting grounds shooting everything that moved, I had come to look on killing as something short of being a good and noble sport.

Oh, I still killed—went out every fall. Then in spring, with a special permit from the Wisconsin Department of Natural Resources, I shot with a high-powered pellet gun some of the hundreds upon hundreds of purple grackles which invaded our four spruce groves to break spires from thousands of tender young trees trying to reach for the sun.

"It's more than that," I said. "None of the girls has ever gone hunting, killed anything. That's part of it."

"What about muskrats? What about mink? What about opossums?"

And Gwen was right. They had and did kill all these. Muskrats because they made our dikes look like slices of Swiss cheese. Mink because every once in awhile one got among their rabbits, ducks, and pigeons and went on a killing spree. And opossums, because there were so many, no duck egg was safe during any spring.

"But it's different," I said. "It's very nearly a survival thing they're doing. Don't kill muskrats and there are no pools to swim and fish in. Don't kill mink and their pets go. Don't kill 'possums, and in spring there aren't any wild ducklings."

"It's still killing."

"Then why don't they let me kill the drake? Why don't they let me kill, for instance, all the songbirds which are injured when they bang up against the windows? Why didn't they let me kill that woodchuck which was so badly burned in that grass fire? Why didn't they . . ."

Gwen had gently put her hand over my mouth. "Easy now," she said. I hadn't realized it, but I had begun to shout. "I don't quite know either just why or how they go about making these distinctions," she said, "but they do, and perhaps if we were a little smarter ourselves, we'd know why."

I eased my head back down on the pillow. Gwen let her hand slip warmly, softly from my lips down to my neck. "It's Sunday," she said. "Relax. Everything will work out."

And, of course, she was right, but that still didn't answer my question. How, for instance, could Debbie be tough enough to stand coolly by and see her yearling horse, Rebel Red, go to his knees and then roll over from the anesthetic the veterinarian had given him. How could she watch unblinking as he cut away the horse's testicles to geld it, and then taking a shovel carry the amputated part to the spruce for burial? And then how, on that very same day, after the dogs had killed a tiny rabbit she'd had only a few days, could she carry around the carcass, and then sit with it in her hands, weeping in the sunken garden until you felt you had to just go out and take it away from her. How?

Why kill a mouse in a feed bin and rescue one from a field? Why willingly and almost greedily eat a crisp, brown wild duck I had brought back from a hunting trip and not savor one which had stepped into a musk-rat trap?

I didn't know, but it had been the same with all of them. The oldest, Sharon, twenty-four at the time Peg Leg Pete came into our lives, had been no different than the youngest who was now eight.

Was it because they had no control over the destiny of those animals and birds which I shot, but did have something to say about the animals and birds which personally crossed their paths? But then how about the muskrats, mink, and 'possums? Whatever it was they were making some extremely fine and certainly bewildering distinctions.

Still, as children, they were united in their decisions. They seemed intuitively to have the same sense of proportion (even if I didn't sometimes know what it was), because they seldom, if ever, disagreed among themselves over the fate of any of the wild ones.

"Anyway," I said to my wife, as we lay there in bed together on that cold December morning, "it was much simpler when I was a boy. We believed all animals were put on earth to serve man. We had few doubts about it, and if we ever did, our parents soon knocked them out of our heads."

"I know. I know," Gwen was soothing me, because my voice had started to lift as the perplexity of my children pricked at me.

"You know what?" I suppose I sounded angry.

"I know one thing," she said. "I know things are changing. Kids, some kids, think differently today. They aren't as convinced as you and I were that all animals were put on earth merely to serve mankind."

Then it all struck me as funny. The kids upstairs talking about the duck's chances for survival. My wife and I talking about old ideas and *their* chances of survival. And the mallard drake lying out there in the cold.

"Hmmph," I said, and maybe I chuckled.

"Hmmph? What?" my wife asked.

"Hmmph, it's almost time for church, and you know how I hate sermons."

"What's that got to do with it?"

"Everything. You've been sounding like a preacher. Let's get up. I'm hungry."

(4

The children were in and out of the duck pen all day Sunday. Toward evening Debbie came into the house and announced, "Well, I got him to eat!"

"How?" I asked.

"When he tries to bite me, I let him bite into a handful of corn. When he gets a piece of corn in his mouth, he swallows it."

I went out with her. Everybody trailed along. She took a fistful of corn and then spread her palm where the duck could jab at it with his bill. The first two times he failed, but on the third jab he got a kernel, and when he swallowed it, we could trace its progress down his throat. On the next jab the corn went flying among the packed leaves on which the drake was lying.

Reaching over to a pail, Debbie took another handful of corn. She managed to get another kernel down the drake's throat.

"Well, it won't be long and he'll be eating," I said.

And my prediction was correct. Within a couple of days the drake was taking corn for himself. Then the children mixed sand and small stones with the corn so his gizzard would get abrasives to digest the food.

On Saturday, with the children all home, we brought the drake into the house and took off the bandages. The stump was healing well. There would be a knob of reddish cartilage. It would become hard as iron from exposure to the air. It would protect the bone.

But if his leg was healing, that side of his body was becoming sore and the feathers were disappearing.

"Try turning him over," I said to Debbie, who had been holding him, "and see if he'll lie on the other side." She did, but he flipped right back to the side on which the leg had been amputated. A dozen times she tried to put him on the other side, and each time he flipped back.

"You know where he'd be best off?" I asked.

"Where?" the children chorused.

"In the water."

"What water?" Dianne asked.

"Where else but Clear Pool or the creek. Everything else is frozen."

"But he'd freeze out there," Gwen said.

I shook my head. "The springs come out of the ground at from forty to nearly fifty degrees. That's why Clear Pool stays open. He'd be a lot warmer in the water than lying in the duck pen."

But the children wouldn't consider it. It would be like turning a child out into the world to fend for himself. I could understand their objections. At least two foxes that we knew of lived in the spruce groves which surrounded Clear Pool. Mink came through as a matter of routine. Hawks watched the pool for any living thing,

24

and sometimes horned owls came all the six miles from the Kettle Moraine area to do a little hunting.

"If only he could walk. If only he didn't have to lie on his side," Mary said.

"Why not make him a leg?" It was Gwen.

At once the children were excited. "Then we could call him Peg Leg Pete," Mary said.

And so that's how the drake got named, and that's how I got into the business of making wooden legs for mallards. The first one I made was out of soft pine. Then I made another out of a hard-rubber eraser. I fashioned harnesses out of old leather boot laces, so that within a week, when we decided the stump was healed enough for a fitting, we were ready.

We tried the pine stump first. After it was strapped in place I tilted Pete upright on the kitchen table. At once he fell back over on his side. A dozen times I set him solidly on his one good leg and the wooden leg. Each time, when support was withdrawn, he fell back over. Then, leaving the leg on, we put him back out into the duck pen. But he refused to use it.

During the week then we tried the leg made from the rubber eraser, and I made two new ones with broader bases, hoping this would help him maintain his balance. But the drake refused to stand on any of his peg legs.

Saturday came, and I said, "It's no use. He won't use a leg."

"Well, what are we going to do?" Gwen asked. I could only shake my head.

Christmas came, and in the excitement, the children's concern for Pete did not dominate their days.

Then it was nineteen hundred and sixty-seven. If Peg Leg had taken only a little of our time, he had been often in our thoughts.

It was clear that something had to be done, and quickly. His right side was becoming raw from lying on it. I was sure, unless we got him on his feet or into a sling of some sort, he could get open sores which would become infected.

What's more, winter was on us with intermittent snow storms, and on some mornings the thermometer plunged below zero. All the ponds, and even Clear Pool, froze, and a flock of twelve ducks had moved up into Watercress Creek, the only open water left.

We saw them every time we crossed the bridge. There were eight mallard drakes, too big to be truly wild ones, and we knew it was because the hen had been of some tame variety which had escaped from a flock owned by a neighbor, Mrs. Sibyll Yug. There was a widgeon hen which had sustained a wing injury in a hunting accident, probably on the Fox River which was less than a quarter of a mile away, and three wild mallard hens who had decided that staying in the north was preferable to the long trip south—so long as there was open water and food.

I was all for putting Peg Leg down on the creek to see if he could forage for himself. In winter, if there was open water, the ducks rarely deserted it for the land. It kept their webs warm, even seeped heat up into their bodies since the temperature of the water would surely be above thirty-two degrees, while the air about might drop to as low as twenty below zero.

I felt certain that it was the creek or the axe, though the children would consider neither alternative. "What

26

then?" I asked. "Hang in a sling the rest of his life? Or swim in a tub in the basement?"

I didn't have to worry about the duck ending up in a washtub in the basement. Gwen loved every living thing, but she could draw lines, and I was sure she'd not tolerate a tubful of duck in a basement already crowded with stack upon stack of fireplace wood which edged up to her work areas around the dryer and washer, around the shower stall and the toilet area, around the water softener and the furnace. No, there was no room for a tub with a duck in it in the basement.

By now, of course, the bandages were off. From time to time, then, we strapped on one or another of the artificial legs hoping the duck might change his mind about trying to get around on a peg leg. But it was no use. When a leg was strapped on, the drake only lay there unblinking, waiting for us to take it off.

I put Vaseline on Pete's sore spots, but it only seemed to make them worse. Feathers surrounding the raw area became less resilient and matted to his skin. I was sure the sores would shortly become ulcerated, and several times, while the children were in school, I was tempted to simply knock the drake over the head, and then when they came home explain that he had died.

Pets which died during the winter when the ground was too frozen for burial, went into boxes which were kept in a shed back of the garage. Frozen solid, they would wait there until spring and graves could be dug. There would be one afternoon given over to funerals, but it was no mass burial, because every animal or bird got the privacy of his own grave.

If I did kill Pete, I could have him in a cardboard box in the shed before they got home from school. They

27

would never know, then, that his death had occurred from anything other than natural causes.

Except I didn't do things like that to my children. I don't know why. It had nothing to do with love. I suspect it had more to do with respect. I think it was because I respected them as people, as persons first, and then as children. Anyway, I couldn't practice such a deception, and if I were going to execute the duck they would know about it beforehand.

Saturday came, and I decided it was time to do something, and though we usually ate a leisurely breakfast at our convenience, this day I saw to it everybody came to the table at the same time.

When we were all seated, I got to it without hedging. "Either we put Peg Leg out of his misery," I said, "or he goes down to the creek to fight it out as best he can."

You can't argue with an ultimatum, so the children only looked down into their cereal bowls and said nothing. Only Gwen looked at me, and she asked, "What are his chances in the creek?"

"I don't know," I said, "except that lying on his side in the duck pen he doesn't have a chance. And unless you want a tub of water in your basement with a duck splashing around in it, the creek is the only other place."

I shouldn't, of course, have put her on the spot by reminding everybody that a tub in the basement might be a solution—at least, until spring. I was sorry as soon as I'd said it, and tried to mend matters by adding, "But I don't want him in the basement. The water would be flying in all directions. Unless you cleaned the tub once a day, it would become a cesspool."

At least on that Saturday, as we sat there at the

28

kitchen table, the weather was on my side. Southerly winds had slipped into the state to produce what we called our "January thaw." The temperature was above freezing. Some water was dripping from the eaves, and crossing the bridge that morning on the way to the post office, I saw that Clear Pool was again free of ice.

When no one spoke, I said, "I think he's got a good chance on the creek. The water is never below freezing. It would buoy him up. His side would heal. He'd get some exercise. There'd be other ducks around if he wanted company." I didn't, however, say that the other drakes might exclude him from the little flock, and if he persisted on trying to join it, they might even try to kill him.

Finally Debbie said, "Well, what else?"

I was getting a little impatient. "You know what else. All of you. The 'what else' is the axe."

The launching was unspectacular. Peg Leg floated a little way, took a few strokes with his one good leg, and then let the current carry him up against a rock, and there, like a bit of feathery debris, he floated.

We stayed for a half hour, and then I suggested that we leave him alone. So we went back up the road to the house, and the children went about their Saturday chores while I got in front of the typewriter to answer mail.

The letters were routine so my mind could wander while I was writing. What kept going through my mind, what bothered me, was why the children couldn't be more casual about Peg Leg Pete. If it had been their first experience with a wounded or sick animal, I might have understood their concern. But they had had sick and injured animals by the score. There had been foxes, opossums, seagulls, ducks of every species, scores of rabbits, many kinds of pigeons, pheasants, hawks, songbirds . . . the list was endless.

I stopped typing, dropped my hands, let them rest on my thighs. Well, at least this—their experience with the sick and injured—was never traumatic. Children can, of course, have some heartrending experiences with animals. Probably the most heartrending for a child is the discovery that animals are at war with one another. Perhaps this experience is sometimes traumatic because this knowledge is never assimilated gradually, but comes in a blinding moment of brutality.

A beloved dog crushes the life out of a soft, furry pet rabbit. A friendly coon kills a pet pigeon. A "tame" seagull pecks the eyes out of a still living pet fish.

Right up to the moment of awful truth, the world of animals is soft and furry and bright-eyed. Then in an instant there is red blood on the white fur.

Still, after the first horrifying experience, the children learn to accept the fact that many animals are natural enemies, yet it seems they cannot accept casually that injury and illness are often the lot of many of their animal and bird friends. No matter how many times it happens, it always remains a very personal matter. You'd think they'd get used to it. But they don't, I thought. You'd think they'd learn to accept such things as inevitable, yet every time a pet dies—whether dog or bluejay, squirrel or mouse—for some unfathomable reason they seemed to blame themselves.

I wondered how they had become what my father would have called "soft shelled." Surely, they couldn't have gotten it from me. I still killed a duck upon occasion from a river blind, or brought home a deer with a rifle bullet in it.

Perhaps the older ones had gotten it from the mother who had died, but the youngest was only three at the time, so it isn't likely she got it from that source. Perhaps from Gwen, the woman who was their mother now. Likely from both. And, likely as not, from living as they did surrounded by animals and birds which asked for nothing except to sing and sleep, eat a little of what no one else hardly wanted, and then pay with a sort of faithfulness which sometimes only childish eyes can perceive.

I finished the mail and then went to the kitchen for coffee. I was letting the steam from a hot cup warm my cheeks when the children came in. "He's gone," Dianne said.

I dressed and went down to the creek with them. The drake wasn't around. But where could he have gone? The creek from its source of bubbling springs to Clear Pool wasn't more than two hundred yards long. Spruce came down to the edge and over the water on one side, and on the other side there was a long hedge of multiflora rose.

"He's got to be somewhere under the spruce," I said. And that's where eventually we found him, way back beneath the thick, green boughs where they came down to within inches of the water.

When we pushed in under with a stick he swam out, and I saw at once he was sinking. Not having been in the water for a considerable period of time, his feathers were without oil, and in fact, it was likely his oil glands were not functioning properly or swiftly enough, and so he was soaking up water like a sponge and ready to go down.

"He'll drown," Debbie said.

"Let's catch him and take him out," Mary suggested.

So we tried to corner him at the bridge, but each time we got close, he propelled himself with his wings and managed to elude us by planing along across the surface of the creek.

For an hour we pursued him, sometimes in the creek, sometimes racing along the bank, sometimes being torn by the multiflora rose thorns, sometimes blindly forcing our way through the thick spruce. But Pete wasn't about to be caught, and though he sank lower and lower, he still managed deftly and with ease to stay out ahead of our lumbering pursuit.

Finally exhausted we all came to the bridge to sit. There wasn't a dry spot on any of us. We were mud right up into our hair.

As we sat the sun went behind the clouds which had been climbing steadily out of the west. The wind came around from out of the south and cut in on us from the north. We shivered. The January thaw was over. We got up and hurried up the road, cold now—cold, hungry, wet and disconsolate, beaten and whipped—up the long road and around the bend and beneath the arching boughs of the great hard maple, and then even before we could get into the house, through the heavy white door, the first few flakes of snow came flicking down hard on our heels as a January storm began to move in.

(5

By the time we had all changed into dry clothes, the
snow was coming down in such a whirl of wind, we
could not see the garage, though it was not more than
one hundred and fifty feet from the house.

The children went out into the storm. There were
still chores to be finished—two horses, three dogs, five
ducks, innumerable rabbits to be fed—and no matter
what the weather, the muskrat traps had to be checked
twice a day lest one or another victim was not immediately drowned and lay suffering in a trap.

But storms never seemed to bother the girls. If anything, they exulted in them. I think they welcomed the
challenge, and soon as chores were done, they had
shovels and were digging pathways.

After supper, when I announced that I was going to
plow out the road, they all decided to come along, Debbie sat in the cab of the four-wheel drive Ford truck we
called Bumpy, and the other two sat on the sand which
was piled in the back. I lowered the big red plow and
with the lights cutting but a short path of brightness out
ahead, began winging the snow left and right.

At the bridge we stopped, and the headlights dimly silhouetted Peg Leg Pete, off to one side, his one good foot on a submerged rock near the creek bank. From time to time he shook himself to be free of the snow, which was coming down so swiftly it put a mantle of white across his back.

Just seeing Pete seemingly oblivious to the storm heightened the children's pleasure, and they howled with delight when the plow hit drifts and snow cascaded over the plow and sliding along the hood crashed into the windshield.

When the road was cleared, I said, "While we're at it, we might as well cut trails from the dog pen to the duck pen and out to the stable. They'll all be filled in by morning, but we'll have our routes marked, and it will make it easier, especially if this snow freezes during the night."

So with the girls alternating to have a time of warming up in the cab with me, we rammed Bumpy along old winter routes, and even the dogs—Brig, Buck, and Eekim—came out of their house into the runs to bark, and when we went by the stable, the horses, Rebel Red and Taffy Candy, came out of stalls which were never closed, to stand staring, as if in disbelief, as we went by in a whirl of snow.

That night we all went to bed tired but without regrets. Once, when I awakened during the night, I went to the window. The storm was over and the moon was shining, and the snow-laden trees shimmered like satin statues—milky white, as if made of the purest marble.

But in the morning, when we stopped the truck on the bridge while plowing, Pete was not there. He could have been, of course, anywhere on Little Lakes because it covers a wide area.

So that the reader may have some idea of what we mean when we write "Little Lakes," let it be understood that it is a series of eight ponds, four of which belong to us, and four of which belong to four neighbors.

The ponds, all spring fed, are strung out loosely along Watercress Creek in a shallow valley like a necklace of eight diamonds. The largest pond, the Mill Pond, covers eight acres. The others vary from a half acre to three acres.

For us, the Ellises, Little Lakes is a rambling white house, on a glacial gravel deposit, and a long slope of grass, which tapers down to the welter of icy springs which feed the ponds.

It was a place of giant elms, but disease took all but a few of them, and now it is populated with spruce, pine, ironwood, maple, linden, oak, ash, birch, poplar, choke cherry, hickory, walnut . . . practically every tree native to Wisconsin.

It is further a place of wild flowers of many colors, and a place where hounds and other dogs have lived and do live, and where there are horses, geese, chipmunks, cardinals, goldfinch, warblers, blue jays, waxwings, raccoons, weasels . . . colonies of birds and families of animals.

Like many a country home, it is a place of sweat, calluses, accidents, and sometimes profanities, but always so much love that it sometimes overflows in tears.

This is the place, then, where Pete had vanished.

After we'd opened all the roads and trails, we left the

truck standing on the bridge and went looking. He was not in the creek, neither beneath the heavy spruce boughs nor where the springs bubbled.

So we went to Clear Pool, which covers perhaps a half acre and is hemmed in by spruce and weeping willow, but he was not there either.

"Well, he could fly," I said.

"But, where would he go?" Debbie asked.

"Maybe south," Mary said. "It's what wild ducks do."

"He wouldn't get far," Dianne said. "Not in the condition he is in."

We went back to the bridge. The little flock of ducks was on the water upstream from us. They were grouped tightly, their necks pulled in, their wings clamped to their bodies, only paddling enough to hold their position in the current.

"I just wonder," I said half to myself and half aloud. All three children waited. "Maybe they chased him."

"But why?" Mary asked.

"I don't quite know," I said, "but I've seen it before."

"Seen what before?" Dianne asked.

"A crippled animal being run from the herd or the flock. An albino not being permitted to join the others, but being forced outside to make it on his own. It happens."

"That's terrible," Dianne said.

"Yes, it is," I agreed, "but even people do it. Sometimes especially people do it."

"How do you mean?" Mary asked.

"He means, Dummy," Debbie said with an abrupt tone to her voice, "that sometimes whites hate blacks and yellows hate whites."

"It's even more than that," I said. "Some people just

can't seem to tolerate anyone with a physical disability, nor can they tolerate the elderly. But mostly, since they'd be criticized for running a cripple or an old person off the streets, they just walk across and down the other side of the street."

"You mean," Mary asked, "the healthy ducks didn't want the crippled duck using their creek?"

"Something like that," I said.

"Well, if that's so, maybe he's close by," Debbie said.

"Maybe," I agreed.

And so we looked, and within five minutes we found him in a snowbank where he'd flown, and was now unable to get enough leverage to get back up in the air again. I picked him up, got a bite on the back of my hand, and carried him back to the bridge.

"Maybe we'd better not put him back in there," Mary said.

"Yes, we must. He'll learn to stay out of their way. That's the way it goes, and perhaps after a while they'll even learn to tolerate him."

"How do you know?" Dianne asked.

"Well, I don't really," I said, "but I've seen albino deer being accepted back into a herd. I saw a squirrel which lost its tail being tolerated by the others after a while. I've heard also that African animals eventually come to tolerate a misfit if it hangs around the herd fringe long enough."

"But what if they don't let him be?" Mary asked.

"Then there'll be time to do something about it." With that I put Peg Leg Pete into the water. Immediately he took a drink. Then he swam to where the submerged rock gave him footing, and perched on his one good leg so the water just barely touched his bottom.

After looking around he began to preen, to put feathers which had gone awry back into place, to distribute oil with his long yellow bill to wing ends so they'd stay dry.

The other ducks did not go near him. In fact, they acted as though he wasn't there.

"He'll learn to stay out of their way," I said.

"But what kind of life is that?" Dianne asked.

"What do you mean?"

"Living alone like that. Always afraid to join the others. Being an outcast."

"Time might change that," I said. "I've seen a lot of changes, and time might change things for Pete, too."

Debbie, who would be a senior in high school next year, couldn't help getting in a little dig: "So says ye olde philosopher," she said, not unkindly.

It was enough to make me laugh at myself. My laughter must have been contagious, because the children began to laugh. When the ducks heard our laughter they quacked, somewhat uncertainly at first, and then loudly just as if there was something to laugh and quack about.

Peg Leg Pete let the quacking and laughing go right over his head. He kept on preening, smoothing down breast feathers, fluffing out wing feathers and then running them through his bill so they were smooth again. In the crystalline water we could see his stump hanging, and the tender end of it was submerged.

"Let's go," I said, "and get some corn."

We put the truck in the garage and Mary ran for a can of corn. When we got back to the bridge I rattled the

38

corn in the can and the ducks in the flock quacked excitedly. So we floundered off the road up the creek to feed them first, and then we came back and where there was a shallow place where trout had rolled the pebbles in building nests, we spread corn for Pete.

"Think he'll eat?" Mary asked.

"I think so. If not today, then tomorrow."

"But what if the other ducks attack him?" she asked.

"Well, he can fly. He'll probably fly out of their way, but I don't think he'll be foolish enough to land again in a snow bank. I think he'll just fly to another part of the creek."

Sunday was slipping away. Tomorrow would be school again. The thought made the children uneasy. I could sense it as we walked up the road with a fiery sunset coloring up the sky behind us.

"I'll keep an eye on him," I said. Though I couldn't hear them sigh, I knew, nonetheless, each of them had. If I was committed to being Pete's guardian, then they knew I would, no matter how much I might tease them about how a crippled duck was nothing but a nuisance, and saying how he'd look much better all brown and crisp and stuffed with onion dressing than standing out there above the dark waters of the creek.

But I didn't tease this night as we walked the road between the high snow banks, perhaps because I was troubled too about how even a flock of ducks can be prejudiced. What's more, maybe there was a residual feeling of guilt, maybe some of my own prejudices were showing through, and I couldn't help remembering how as a boy in the fourth grade I had joined a mob to chase another boy because his parents spoke nothing but German, and he spoke broken English.

I wondered where it all stemmed from, this pack security syndrome needing to be fed, reinforced, solidified by zeroing in upon the unfortunate, upon those who couldn't quite conform.

Peg Leg Pete was no threat to the other ducks. Or was he? Would there be less food during this cold winter because there was one more gizzard to satisfy? But, if that was so, why didn't the healthy ducks war among themselves? Why didn't they compete?

But, of course, they did. But they were all of about the same strength, the same adroitness, so they had come to an impasse and were literally forced to tolerate one another.

We were almost to the house when Mary said, "I hate to think of Pete being down with those other ducks. It isn't fair."

I didn't really know what to say to an eight-year-old about something which perplexed even me. So I said, "Well, maybe it'll make him tough. Perhaps in the end he'll turn out to be the best of the lot, better able to survive anything nature can throw his way. It works that way sometimes."

Now the sun had set. We came to the end of the road and turned onto the shoveled sidewalk. I could see Gwen waiting at the door. She motioned toward the basement. Then I could hear her: "You're all snow. Undress downstairs."

We went down the steps past the sun porch and turning went into the outside basement door. My glasses steamed up. I could smell cooking. The children were giggling again—about something.

40

(6

Peg Leg did adjust. He learned to stay clear of the other ducks. His feathers became well oiled and waterproof. He managed, after a while, to swim a fairly straight course. He picked corn from the shallows, rested with his one good leg firmly planted on the submerged rock, and found enough gravel along the shore for his gizzard.

But he never appeared to be happy, and it made the children sad to see him swimming along, all hunched up as if even his feelings like his feathers were curling in on themselves. The other ducks dove and sported around in the water. They clamored when one of us came with corn and made it rattle in the can. Sometimes the flock would lift from the water to make a brief circle in the air before planing back down to the creek. But not Pete. He looked disconsolate.

We could understand, of course, why he might feel sad. He was at a severe disadvantage. He couldn't walk. The water had to forever be his habitat. What's more he could not tip up on end to probe bottoms and sift the silt through his bill looking for succulent morsels, and if there is anything a mallard does better than any other duck, it is tipping up on end.

Then came March, the month of Agony and Ecstasy. The month of promise. It was the year of nineteen hundred and sixty-seven, and our spirits soared with the temperature, only to be buried again by snowstorms. But if the month was marked by bitter days, still all things were progressing toward such freedom as only a resurrection ensures.

Soon, then, there were hepatica, pale blue and in hidden places, and a rash of the first, tiny sweet-smelling purple violets which precede the larger blooms. Green began to thread through last year's dead brown grass, especially where these grasses wet their roots along pond edges.

But, as March can be, it was a month of irony. One day the glades at Little Lakes were so sprinkled with anemones it looked like the Milky Way had spilled over out of the sky. Then the next day a wash of snow would sift down to compete with brush strokes laid on the land by the flowers.

Relentlessly, however, life stretched, unfolded. Up from the tomb of black and suffocating mud, the turtle. Still lethargic, a woodchuck warmed himself in the sun at the mouth of his dungeon.

Now sun seekers all. Green garter snake on the warm top of an overturned pail. Bumblebee, black and yellow bloom on the tip of a tall, dead, last year's thistle. Black ants slow to the warm sidewalk and then, in seconds, scurrying. Unblinking frog on a warm white stone. Low hovering haze of just hatched flies. Sunfish up to the last watery inch with fins out in the air feeling for warmth.

Perhaps I appreciated it much more than the children. Likely it is because not always have I lived in the country as they have, and I can remember a day on a Chicago skid row when spring's entire reflection was in the golden eye of a single dandelion in a junk car grave-yard.

On sunny days during this spring, the whole flock of ducks would leave the creek and settling over their webs, tuck their bills beneath their wings and sleep on the warm banks. Peg Leg tried once that I saw, but he couldn't make it. Each time he clambered a little way up the bank he fell back, and then finally he gave up and finding another submerged rock where the sun came down between the alley of spruce, multiflora rose and other vegetation which held the creek, he perched there and slept.

Then one day, the day the geese came over, the flock moved out, swam down the creek into Clear Pool, climbed the bank and waddled across the dike and through the marsh to where the current had cut a big V of open water out into the crumbling ice of Mill Pond. I can't forget the day because I can't forget any day when the geese play their sweet flutes of freedom from the want of winter.

So Peg Leg was the only duck on the creek, and sometimes trespassing boys paused to throw stones at him, and one gray morning while on my way to the post office, I saw one of the foxes which lived on the place standing with his forefeet in the creek—head down, almost drooling—as Pete swam a safe distance away, and paddling idly to maintain his position, watched.

Then, the blackbirds came back, males first, and they sat among the cattails and their cheering was some-thing to hear when the first females began to arrive.

43

The cardinals sat on the spruce spires and among the highest branches of the hard maples and whistled so piercingly, the two horses in the pasture whinnied impatiently, because it was the children's habit to whistle loudly as they walked from the house to the stable at feeding time.

The children were swept along with the changing seasonal tide, but they found time to pause on the bridge, and as children are wont to do, talk to the crippled duck as though he were another human and could understand what it was they were saying.

Then Taalon and Teelon, the red-shouldered hawks, came back to their nest in the giant dead elm, victim of the Dutch elm disease. The gigantic tree stood on the shores of Fish Pond, and though we had cut down most of the other dead elms to prevent the spread of the disease, we were reluctant to drop this one because of the nest.

So every day now as the weeks became warmer, I went with my pellet gun to where hundreds of purple grackles had gathered among the spruce groves, and each day I shot four.

The hawks would scream when they saw me come from the house with the gun, and then sail quietly in circles until I put the dead birds down on a stump. If the hawks were very hungry they would eat right there on the stump. Otherwise they would fly to the elm with the birds and resting on a large limb, and while holding the birds firmly in their talons, strip away the dark, red meat.

It was a sacrifice of sorts. Four grackles to keep peace, to keep the hawks from molesting any and all of the other birds and animals which gravitated to Little Lakes.

And it worked, until the grackles became scarce, and until there were young in the nest to feed, and then sometimes we had to sacrifice a cottontail because they wouldn't eat the carp we caught for them in the Mill Pond, nor would they eat the scraps of meat we put out. Instead then, they turned to, of all things, the small black, corrugated snapping turtles with which Fish Pond abounded.

They caught them easily enough while the turtles were sunning, and they unhinged their armor plating quite effortlessly, and sad to say, sometimes got on with their feasting even before the little amphibians were dead. Finished, they dropped the shells, and soon, under various trees, there was quite a collection of snapping turtle half-shells, all neatly cleaned out.

But, as during the previous year, once the young were born they extended their hunting range, and then if there weren't any turtles or frogs or crayfish or mice . . . they weren't above taking a songbird, and then one day I saw the female hawk make a pass at Peg Leg.

In the morning I saw her from the house circling near the bridge. It occurred to me then that perhaps she was looking the duck over, considering in what way she could successfully convert him into a meal. I went back in, however, because I had a column to write, but when I came back out for my noon break, she was still circling.

The children were in school, of course, so I went down off the low hill on which the house stands, and keeping to the spruce which edge the road, came to

45

where I could get a view of both the creek and the hawk.

As I had suspected, she was stalking Peg Leg. He was floating on the creek surface, turning his head from time to time to put an eye on the big bird, but otherwise making no sound, nor making any effort to get away.

Red-shouldered hawks, of course, are not the great hunters of the hawk family. There are other species more adept at making swift killing dives. Mostly the red-shouldered hawks like to sit in the low trees above any marshy place, looking for frogs, mice, young muskrats . . . prey which isn't likely to fight back.

But they will and they can come like a bolt of lightning to take a rabbit on the run and slam him so hard with their balled talons they break his back. They are well equipped to kill with strong, sharp, curved beaks and iron-hard talons with the grip of a vise.

Their wingspan is sometimes more than three feet, but rather than savage killers, they are mostly patient birds willing to wait for the precise moment when they can make a strike and a kill with a minimum of effort.

Still I was sure the hawk had designs on Peg Leg. There was nothing else in sight. It had to be the duck, but she was probably wary of the way in which the spruce and the multiflora came to the water, afraid she might crack up during a dive.

In ways it was fascinating to watch. The hawk so patient. The duck seemingly so unperturbed. The sunshine on the hawk's wings and the water below. The reflection of the creek in the duck's eye. The spruce, glowing with new growth. The multiflora, caught up in a green haze of new leaves.

This was the second year the hawk pair had been

with us. Last year I had never seen them so much as eye any of the ducks which were fairly plentiful. So, perhaps they knew Peg Leg was a cripple, that he was vulnerable.

A healthy duck on being dive-bombed by a hawk will usually dive, and that's the end to that. Pete, of course, couldn't dive. So I have to believe that either the hawk's keen eyes had noticed that the leg was missing, or she knew something was wrong because the duck was always alone, and when he swam, he went along at a slight angle having to correct from time to time to stay on course.

I suppose I should have gone down to the creek and waved the hawk off. The bird would have left if I had inserted myself between her and the duck. But I felt that I would only be postponing things, so I stayed there, partly concealed by spruce, and waited.

I didn't have to wait long. The male hawk, perhaps an eighth of a mile away in the elm made a shrill sound, and it precipitated the female into action. Flying up the creek so she could slant down its length, she tipped up, and with wings partly folded, started her stoop.

It was only a short dive, and she didn't get the momentum she might have gotten from a longer stoop from greater altitude. Still, by the time she was a few feet off the water, she was traveling so fast I didn't see how Pete could get out of her way.

But he did get out of her way. With a flop of his wings, he darted to one side, and in the next instant he was airborne. He flew strongly almost straight up, and then at a height of about fifty feet, leveled off. He flew across Clear Pool, lifted to clear the billowing willows, and then slanted down in the direction of Fish Pond.

47

Meanwhile Teelon almost came to grief against the sides of the bridge. Trying desperately to pull out of her dive, to check her speed, she put her talons straight out and cupped her wings. But the impetus of her dive carried her right up to the bridge, and the only thing which saved her was that at the last second she changed the angle of her wings so she glided just up and over the planks.

Having righted herself, she flew into a small basswood and began preening as though nothing had happened.

I turned to look in the direction Peg Leg Pete had flown, but I could not see him. So I came out from under the spruce and taking a shortcut around New Pool, came to the shores of Fish Pond, and there sat Peg Leg, almost directly under the hawk's nest.

From the frying pan into the fire, I thought. While I stood there Teelon came back. Taalon welcomed her with a brief cry, and then the pair began circling the crippled duck.

By now I was convinced that they knew of Peg Leg's deformity, of his inability to dive beneath the surface of the water to save himself. I was sure they'd never have singled him out from all the other ducks if they hadn't realized that he was vulnerable.

Fish Pond was too big, of course, for me to mount any kind of counter offensive against the hawks, other than interfering with firearms, and that I didn't intend doing. There might have been a chance of distracting the hawks had I quickly shot them each a grackle, but even that might only postpone what obviously had to end in some sort of climactic confrontation. The best I could hope for was some kind of impasse.

So I climbed a knoll and sat where I could look down on the duck and the two hawks which were cautiously circling and calling out to each other from time to time. I thought that they were perhaps trying to panic the duck into making a move, but if they were, Pete wasn't about to fall for it.

When the attack came, I could see there was a plan of sorts, a strategy which obviously the hawks had used before. Taalon flew a shorter circle so he was always directly above Pete, and Teelon flew off to one side so when she dove she would drive the duck back into the bank.

I'm sure, if they didn't mentally plan it, it was an intuitive thing the species had worked out over the years.

Pete must have realized the trap was closing. He swam more swiftly in circles, keeping one eye on each of the birds waiting for them to make their move.

I don't know if the hawks had a signal to start the action. I didn't hear anything, but suddenly Teelon was gliding down and when Pete started to lift from the water, Taalon, who was just above, lowered himself to be in a position to strike.

It was the old squeeze play, and Pete dropped back down and began scooting toward the bank by propelling his wings like oars. Then in an instant the female hawk was on him, had him pinned up against the bank.

But that didn't end it as I expected it would. What happened next went too swiftly for my eyes to catalogue. But there was a flurry of wings and feathers went flying. I heard Pete quack once, and then as the action slowed down, I could see he was striking out at the hawk with his hard bill and hard wing elbows.

Time and again the hawk lifted a few feet off the ground so she could descend and deliver the fatal blow, but each time Pete was ready with his devastating wing thrusts and hard, drilling blows of his bill. In the end Peg Leg bested her, and she flew a few feet away and sat on the bank looking at him as though not able to understand how it was she couldn't kill this duck.

Above Taalon screamed as though urging her to renew the attack. But she looked spent, her head low, her wings spread as though for balance, her rapacious bill snapping as though in anger.

Then when Pete swam away toward the center of the pond, Teelon gave a hop and was airborne. With Taalon, she returned to the dead elm. Then together they sat on a low branch watching while Peg Leg preened his feathers back into place.

Good for you, Peg Leg, I said to myself. Good for you. And with that I went to the house for the pellet gun to kill some grackles for the hawks, because I was sure they wouldn't be eating duck—not Peg Leg Pete, anyway.

（7

Even before the ice went out, the three wild mallard
hens had accepted drakes. The pairing had not come,
however, until after several weeks of fighting. There
had been much chasing, both in the air and on the
water, and sometimes we could hear the drakes all the
way up to the house. Some days they battled so long
that finally exhausted they lay on the water with wings
spread and bills open, gasping for air.

To watch drakes fight, is to suddenly discover that
ducks, especially mallards, are capable of acrobatics. It
comes as a surprise, since mallards seem to labor to
maintain even normal flight. But when the mating season approaches, and the scramble for dominance takes
to the air, the mallards can execute maneuvers which
are clearly scintillating.

Though I've observed mallards and other ducks all
my life, I don't know at what moment, or by what
special dint of effort, the pairing is finally decided. All
I know is that quite suddenly it is all over, the pairing
had been decided, and the newly joined swim off to be
by themselves, while what drakes are left over become

friends again and float around in a bachelor colony seemingly as content as before the fighting began.

The three hens, of course, disappeared, so we knew that egg laying had finally been accomplished, and they were incubating. Sometimes, very early in the morning or late in the evening, we might see them come for water or to take a little corn. They would appear irritable, look blowzy, and were always in a hurry. After a drink, and eating perhaps only several kernels of corn, they would hurry back to where the nests were on high ground, likely beneath a spruce, or in a hay field, or along a fence line next to a leaning post.

As was their custom, now that spring was warming, the children took Gertie, Waddle, Greta, Aristotle, and Plato from their pens on the hill down to the pond we called Blue Pool so they could enjoy a swim.

After swimming, they would carry the wet ducks up the hill and put them back behind wire. If one or another eluded capture, they let him or her stay, and then, almost always, the reluctant one would find his own way back and that night or the next morning be standing in front of the gate waiting to be let in.

One day when Gertie refused to let one of the children close enough to pick her up, she was left behind. Then when she wasn't at the gate the next morning, they went down to Blue Pool looking for her. It was a Sunday, and I was in my big, brown leather chair reading the paper, when I heard them at the back door.

"Dog! Dog!" They often called me "Dog" instead of "Dad." It was a mark of extreme affection, a compliment of the highest order, because there were few creatures in the world so wonderful as the three dogs they kept in the white kennel back near the lot line.

I got up and went through the dining room into the kitchen. Dianne and Mary were standing on the mud rug in the sun-room because they knew it was against the house rules to come farther unless they had their boots off.

"Guess what?" Mary said.

"Let me tell it," Dianne interrupted.

"Calm down. Both of you," I said.

"Gertie's got a mate," they said it together.

"And guess who it is," Dianne said.

Of course, I couldn't guess. The fact that Gertie had taken a mate was enough to ponder on, at least for the moment.

Dumpy Gertie, though often courted, had never been wed. Nobody knew why, but down through the years she had each spring refused the advances of any and all. So to think that at this late date Gertie had mated seemed a little doubtful.

Like Peg Leg, Gertie had come from a muskrat trap. But there had been no injuries, except to two toes. One morning while Walter Hanley was running his trap line in a marsh near Sun Prairie, Wisconsin, which is seventy-five miles from Little Lakes, he found her.

Since he didn't know from what barnyard flock she might have come, he took her home, and then he gave her to Dianne. This was before I was Dianne's dad, because I hadn't yet met and married her widowed mother. So when, after my other wife had been dead awhile, and I brought Gwen and Dianne out to live at Little Lakes, of course, Gertie came along.

That very first year we presented Gertie with a procession of drakes, but she spurned them all. We tried tempting her with many species, including Rouen, Pekin, Muscovy, and partly wild mallards. Gertie warded off all amorous advances.

This peculiar duck behavior might have been more humanly understandable if Gertie had been a sleek, beautiful woodduck, or a svelte pintail, or even a shy mallard hen. Then there might have been some reason for her being picky, choosy.

But, let's face it, Gertie was an out-and-out fatty. I'm sure I don't know how she looked to other ducks, but to a human she couldn't have looked anything except ludicrous. Even her feet were funny. They were big as soup ladles. Then when Gertie waddled, her rear end was so low down it brushed the grass, and she seemed to have trouble getting it over even such a little obstacle as an acorn.

Yet, she must have had something, because the drakes pursued her. Of course, her coloring was beautiful. She had white feathers and their tips ended in a soft, golden hue, so there seemed to always be an aura of sunshine about her.

Anyway, whatever it was that had made drakes desirous of her, it hadn't mattered, because she sent some mighty handsome specimens—many pure white with glowing red crests—back to a corner of the pen where they sulked dejectedly. And, despite their sometimes relentless pursuit, Gertie remained a virgin.

So I wondered who the lucky suitor might have been. "Well, who is it. Tell me. Who did Gertie mate with?" I asked, as the two girls and I headed for Blue Pool.

"It's Peg Leg Pete," the two girls said, as though they'd rehearsed it together.

"Peg Leg Pete! Peg Leg Pete?" It couldn't be that cripple. The drake least likely to survive. The drake who couldn't even get along in a bachelor colony. Gertie had accepted him? I couldn't believe it, and I said, "Well, I'll have to see it before I believe it."

As we neared Blue Pool the girls slowed their pace. "Shhh. Go quiet. You'll scare them," Dianne warned.

We stopped beneath an oak with a corrugated trunk and great branches which age and weight had brought low so we were in a bower of leaves. It was a good place to see what was going on on Blue Pool without being seen.

Well, they were together, side-by-side, like an old married couple. Pete was bobbing his head like a drake husband should, and Gertie was clucking softly and edging up to him.

"See, I told you," Mary whispered.

"I still don't believe it. Did you actually see them mate?"

"Yes, we saw them," Dianne said.

"But he . . . he's only half her size."

"Well they did it. Right in the water," Mary said.

So how do you explain females? Even female ducks? Here she'd had the pick of a long line of handsome drakes and now, in what must be her dotage, she picked an outcast, a cripple.

"But Gertie's got to be seven or eight years old," I said.

"What's wrong with that?" Mary asked. "Look at Mom and you. There's a pretty big difference in your ages."

And so there was, seventeen years. "But it's the other way around in our case," I said. "I'm the old one and she's the young one, and sometimes it works well that way. But when the female is in the October of her life,

55

and the male is still enjoying his springtime . . ." I threw up my hands.

"Maybe to ducks that doesn't matter," Mary said.

"It shouldn't matter with people either," Dianne said.

"Maybe it shouldn't," I agreed, and then added, "but very often it does."

"Does what?" Dianne asked.

"Make a difference."

"Well it shouldn't. Not if they're in love."

Of course, there never is a good answer when you bring love into anything, so I just said, "Well, I just don't believe the two are really mated."

"But we saw them," Mary insisted.

Then just as if to prove the girls were right, Gertie sank low in the water, and Pete hopped onto her back, and in an instant the mating was consummated.

"Well, I never!"

"See. Didn't I tell you," Mary said.

"Let's leave them alone," Dianne said. "It just doesn't seem fair to be watching."

We backed away carefully, quietly. Then when we were back near the house, I said, "You'd better get some corn down there for them."

Gertie stayed down on Blue Pool for nearly ten days, and then one morning she was back at the gate of the duck pen wanting in. The children let her in, and within minutes she was busy gathering dry grass, bits of straw and hay, and a few dead leaves for her nest.

She built the nest in a small nail keg, one of several which stood around convenient for any female in residence who might from time to time require one.

When she laid her first egg, you'd think Christmas

had arrived, or it was somebody's birthday, or summer vacation was about to begin.

"They'll not be fertile," I predicted. "Nothing will come of it."

The children stood there looking at me as if I had just announced the end of the world. Finally Debbie said, "Why shouldn't they be fertile?"

"Gertie's too old," I said.

But what I thought didn't faze Gertie. She went right on laying an egg a day until she had five, and most mornings Peg Leg Pete would fly up from the pool and whisking overhead quack solemnly as he turned an eye down on her.

Gertie was a good sitter. She never stayed off the eggs more than a few minutes at a time, and even when she took a brief interlude for food and water, she carefully covered the nest of white eggs with down from her breast.

Then when nearly a month was up, and a mottled black and yellow duckling squirmed from an egg, all of Little Lakes rocked with excitement. During that same day another duckling was born, and Mary wanted to sit with Gertie that night to see her through the birth of the other three.

I would have let her because I usually let the children do what they want to do if it isn't too dangerous, and if it won't hurt them in other ways.

But a thunderstorm came up, and Mary came into the house soaked to the skin. After she had changed clothes, she wanted to take an umbrella and go back out.

"No, Gertie is in a protected place. She won't get wet."

"But Susie sat with her duck while it rained."

And that was a fact. Some years before, Susie her sister (gone off and married now) had held an umbrella over one of her mallards during a thunderstorm while the eggs were hatching.

"But Susie's duck was sitting out in the open. She had no protection. Your duck is in a barrel."

The thunder cracked then, and perhaps it lent emphasis to my words, because Mary desisted.

All that night the rain came down, and gusts of wind tore branches from the trees, and sometimes the lightning was so bright we could see all the way down to where the ponds gleamed. Twice the electricity went off, and the children went often to the picture window to see if, by the lightning's bright flashes, they might see the duck pen through the grove of spruce which surrounded it.

Sometime before dawn the storm passed on, and a bright sun came up to look on a brightly washed world. Mary was outside before the others. I heard her come downstairs, heard the sun-room door open and close. Then I heard her come back in, and then there was a rap at our bedroom door.

"You should have let me sit with them," she said, coming into the bedroom. She had been crying.

"Why?" I asked. "What's the matter?"

"Three died. Three little ducks died."

And she was right. Three more had hatched, and of the five, three had strayed from the nest and being pelted by rain and wind had died in the mud outside the barrel.

"I'm sorry, Mary," I said, "but you just couldn't have sat up all night with them. Not in that storm."

58

"Then we should have brought them in."

"Well, maybe we should have," I said. "Just maybe we should have. But how do you know?"

The two surviving ducklings stayed beneath Gertie's wings until the sun was high and warm. The children had gone off to school. Mary's rancor toward me, if there had been any, dissolved, because she knew there was nothing we might have done, that it was just one of those things which happen when you have a lot of pets.

I was next to the duck pen when the pair came out. One was black and yellow. The other was mostly yellow. I was sure the yellow would someday turn to white.

When I went back into the house I said to Gwen, "I just can't believe it."

"You can't believe what?"

"Well, first off, the mating between Gertie and Pete, and secondly, how a duck as old as Gertie has got enough of everything that is necessary to manufacture eggs."

"How about Sarah?"

"Sarah? Sarah who?"

"The biblical Sarah. The one who, in her old age, surprised everybody by giving birth."

"Well, I don't believe that either."

"That's because you underestimate us women," Gwen said, with a mischievous smile.

"Not any more," I said, "not any more I don't."

(8

Any residual grief Mary might have felt over the death of the three ducklings was quickly forgotten when she and Dianne found seven helpless kingfishers during that July of nineteen hundred and sixty-seven.

The birds, born at the end of a long, dark bank tunnel, had come out, and when the children found them they were neatly lined up at the edge of the water chirring for a parent.

The birds were so weak they could only remain upright by bracing long, black beaks to the ground. The girls searched for the parents, and then finally had to bring the fledglings home.

They force fed the youngsters fish, but on each of two succeeding nights two died. On the third morning, however, the three survivors were more than willing to eat the tiny green sunfish and bluegills the girls caught for them.

Not born for walking, but to perch and then fly swift and piercing as an arrow, the blue youngsters were awkward and clumsy on the ground. So as the youngsters became stronger, the children took them for trial flights.

Eventually then, the three kingfishers learned to dive with unerring accuracy to spear their own fish, and ultimately, though for two years they came back to visit, the orphans were dependent on no one.

But that's another story, and I'm getting ahead of myself. Once Gertie's and Pete's ducklings hatched, true to form, Peg Leg evinced no further interest in the hen or his offspring.

Gertie's kids grew swiftly. One was almost all black, and the other about half black and half white. But both had hints of green, blue, and brown shading into and along the edges of their black and white parts. By the end of summer it was obvious they were both drakes and would be bigger than Peg Leg, but not so big as their mother.

Earlier, the Pekin had mated with the Muscovy, and they had eight yellow, fluffy offspring, and so territories were established, and if one duckling chased a fly across established, though invisible, boundary lines, anxious mothers herded them back to territorial safety.

All of which had nothing to do with Pete. He was flying regularly now—especially mornings and evenings—and if he lacked dexterity on the ground or in the water, he made up for it with dazzling bursts of speed in the air.

"Think he'll go south?" Debbie asked one day, as we stood on the wide sweep of lawn which comes down to the ponds.

I looked across to where Pete had just executed an abrupt climb to get up and over a billowing weeping willow, and I said, "I don't know, Debbie." Then I thought about it, and I added, "But I can tell you this much, I am sure hoping that he doesn't. He might run into trouble with only one leg."

We were standing near the hawk tree. The three red-shouldered hawk youngsters had left the nest of sticks the day before, but they were only making experimental flights from one limb to another, and the old ones were still feeding them.

"How many of the ducks do you think will go south?" Debbie asked.

There were perhaps two dozen ducks on the ponds now, counting young of the year. One wild mallard hen hadn't been able to bring off a hatch. Though she tried three separate times, opossums got the eggs each time.

The other two hatched twelve and ten, respectively, but out of the twenty-two many had fallen prey to snapping turtles, the hawks, mink . . . and one day I saw a big trout in Clear Pool take one down when it swam clear of the clutch.

But that was the way with life at Little Lakes, and if you were going to police the inhabitants (which we sometimes did in the beginning), then you might starve a litter of young mink because you killed a marauding mother, or you might let a hawk's eggs grow cold and lifeless because you shot the female to protect the cardinals . . . so in the end, we decided against making any moral judgments of our neighbors and let nature's laws of survival decide most issues.

As I've said, only sometimes did we interfere, like when muskrats threatened to let everything go down the drain by ventilating the dikes, or when 'possums got so thick they were on the verge of stalking one another, or when hordes of grackles broke the tender leaders on the spruce, or when a feral cat got so good at the business of killing he did it mostly for the excitement.

Debbie's question about migration was one which came up every year. Now as we walked between Fish Pond and Blue Pool to come to the edge of Mill Pond, where most of the ducks lived in summer, she asked still another question: "What determines which ducks go south and which stay behind."

I thought about it as we walked and found I had no ready answer as to how many would migrate or which ones would make the trip. Finally I said, "Partly, I think, migration depends on how wild the duck is. If there's lots of domestic duck been bred into an individual, he's likely to stay. Then usually the ones that have been injured or crippled stay."

Often in fall wounded ducks and geese came up from the Fox River where hunters had blinds, and many of these would stay the winter, and then perhaps leave in spring—or maybe even become permanent residents.

"Then likely Pete will stay around." Debbie made it half question, half statement of fact.

"I don't know."

"But you said the crippled usually stay."

"Sure, but I hardly think of Pete as a cripple any more."

We had come to the shores of Mill Pond. The little bay into which Watercress Creek emptied had many ducks on it. Most were back among the willows along the far shore near Mrs. Yug's place, or among the cattails. Many were sleeping. Some few were feeding, but without enthusiasm.

"They're molting," I said.

63

"How long does the molt take?" Debbie asked.

"I don't quite know. It's a kind of gradual thing. Seems they start losing some old feathers early in summer and getting some new ones at the same time. Except about now (it was August) they don't have quite enough flight feathers to become airborne."

"They look it, too," Debbie said.

And they did. They looked tacky. The bright mating colors of spring had faded. They looked splotchy, like a woman in the process of removing her makeup.

"I noticed the hens don't call much during the summer," Debbie said.

"That's right. Usually they've got young, and they'd rather not call attention to themselves. But wait until the nights get crisp and the lawn gets white with its first frost. Then you'll hear them sound off."

"There he is," Debbie pointed.

And, sure enough, it was Pete, sitting off all by himself on a half-submerged willow trunk which grew right out the side of the bank so it was partly submerged. Even while we watched he hopped off the sloping tree trunk and began to swim toward the marsh.

"He's still pretty jerky," Debbie said.

"Well, who wouldn't be with only one leg."

"Think he might get shot this fall?"

I shrugged. We figured at least a third of the ducks which summered with us would get shot when the hunting season opened. By then they'd all be making flights as far as the river, and every year a certain number had to be killed before the others seemed to realize that safety for them lay in staying on the ponds which were within the village boundaries, and therefore off limits to hunters.

64

Though all the ducks we saw were in small family flocks or bachelor colonies, Pete was alone.

"Don't you think he'll ever be accepted by the others?" Debbie asked.

"That's a question I can't answer."

"But you'd think they'd get used to having him around."

"I don't know. It doesn't work that way. Not even with people."

"Maybe it's him," Debbie said. "Maybe he doesn't want any part of them."

"Could be."

"But why?"

I had to laugh. "Debbie, if I knew all the answers to all the questions you kids ask, I'd probably be just about the smartest guy in the world. Then I wouldn't be here. Not at Little Lakes. I'd be 'President of the World,' and I'd be solving the problems of poverty, pollution, war, racism, disease . . ."

Debbie laughed. Then solemnly, she asked, "Do you think a leader like that might ever come along? I really mean it. Someone all the world could respect? A man smart enough and kind enough to show the people the way out of all their troubles?"

"It'd be a miracle," I said.

Pete had paddled so close we could see the gleam in his eye.

"He looks like a tramp," Debbie said. "What I mean is, he looks so sort of patchy. His green head isn't green anymore. The canvas colors on his back are all checkered. He really looks down and out."

"But he isn't," I said. "It's only the molt. Give him another month or two, he'll look magnificent again."

"Do you think he knows how he looks?"

"I rather doubt it. I just suppose that a lot of his energy is going into growing new feathers, and he probably doesn't feel as chipper as he might with all those bodily changes taking place."

"Say, you sure know a lot about ducks."

"Not really, Debbie. A lot of it is guesswork. I've never really studied them like some naturalists have. I only watch them, and maybe some of my guesswork is right, and maybe some of it is wrong."

"Well, you sure make sense."

"Thanks. Except you shouldn't take my word for everything. Just use my words as a starting point to go on from, to learn more."

"Now you sound stuffy, like a teacher I don't like."

Loud quacking ended Debbie's analysis of me. Pete had ventured too close to a clutch of pin-feathery youngsters, and the old hen was propelling herself across the water quacking with indignation, and Pete was planing out ahead trying to get away.

"I'd fight back," Debbie said.

"Not if you were a man you wouldn't."

"What's that got to do with it?"

"How'd you like to see me hit a woman?"

"I don't suppose I'd like it. But if she hit you, I think you should have the right to belt her right back."

"Women's Lib?"

"Maybe. I suppose. If a woman wants things the same as a man, I suppose she should expect to get belted once in a while."

I laughed. "Maybe you're right. But what about us

old guys who couldn't hit a woman even if our lives depended on it?"

"You're probably social cripples. Just like Pete. You're victims of the Victorian mess."

I laughed again. Then Debbie laughed. Peg Leg heard our laughter and he raised his head high to see where the sound was coming from.

"You wouldn't really want to see me slug a woman? Even if she deserved it?"

"No, not really," Debbie said, and she put a hand on my arm.

The sun was low now, and we were looking right into it. Behind us Mary and Dianne were in the cooling waters of Blue Pool, splashing and shouting.

I couldn't look across the water any longer. The sun was too blinding, so I turned my back on the Mill Pond. Debbie turned too.

"You know," she said, as we started up the slight incline to where the other two children were swimming, "animal and bird customs seem to follow human patterns. Or maybe that's putting it backward. Maybe I should say, man's customs seem to follow those of the birds and the animals."

"Now you're getting into deep water," I said. "Remember there's a spider female which eats her mate right after the honeymoon. And remember there are bull elks with harems, and there are lion societies where the females do all the hunting and killing. So you can't generalize."

"I suppose not. But I always look for human traits in animals and birds."

"That's natural. And when you find a human trait in animals or birds you feel closer to them, and it makes it easier to identify with them, and that's the beginning of compassion, and maybe even love."

"Wow!"

"Wow? Wow what?"

"We're really getting into things now."

"Well, you're old enough. You're sixteen. Soon you'll be in college. It's time you looked beneath the surface."

"But it sometimes scares me."

"Well, if it's any comfort to you, I'm three times as old as you are, and let me tell you, sometimes it scares me, too."

The children in the pool saw us and began shouting for us to join them. Gwen was coming down the slope of the lawn from the house wrapped in a beach towel, so we knew she was going swimming.

"Let's go swimming," Debbie said, starting to run for the bathhouse where the swimming suits were hung.

When we were in the water, Debbie swam close to me. "Say," she said. "You know if you're going to look at the similarities in birds, animals, and man, I suppose you ought to include fish."

It was still on her mind, so I knew her carefree days were ending. That from here on out, from time to time, she'd be troubled by those mysteries beyond comprehension.

"Just don't let it get you," I said.

"Oh, it won't," she replied, splashing water in my direction.

"That's good."

"Except, I think you're just a little wrong in some ways."

"How's that?"

"Well, actually there are women who, like the spider,

68

eat their husbands. If not literally, then figuratively—they consume them. And there are women who, like the lion females, do all the hunting and all the work for the whole family all their lives. And there are some guys, just like the bull elk, who have more women on the string than you can shake a stick at."

"I get the message," I interrupted.

"Good," she laughed, and with the palm of her hand shot a stream of water into my face. I choked and sputtered.

That night, after the children were in bed, Gwen and I got on the subject of animal "personalities" again. We had both just finished reading Mary McCarthy's *Birds of America* (which is not about birds, but migrating Americans). In the book, one of Mary McCarthy's characters avers that only domestic, or "tame," wild animals develop personalities, but that the wild ones conform to such a set pattern there is no way of telling one from the other.

"Of course," I said, "that's wrong." I went on to explain to Gwen that there are, for instance, lazy mountain lions and industrious mountain lions. I added that there were peaceful robins and belligerent robins, sagacious bunnies and dumb bunnies.

"There are even orioles who do not seem to have the skill to build a proper nest, and when the wind tatters it, their nests look like remnants from a rummage sale," I added.

"But how can you be sure?" she asked.

"Well in my experience hunting deer," I continued, "I have never seen two bucks that have lived long enough to acquire sizable racks (sets of antlers) that didn't each have idiosyncrasies that set them apart.

"By the same token, some foxes are patient parents while others push their youngsters from the den too soon and lose them. Crows especially run the personality gamut. Even in the wilds it is possible to tell one from the other by their actions. Even fish have individual water and food preferences. It's wrong to think wild ones are mass produced like bottle caps because mice, even as men, are as different as the stars even if a precursory look would indicate they are all made of the same shining dust."

With that we went into the bedroom and to bed.

9

Summer lingered that year. It was still warm and the maples were still scarlet when the guns began to boom along the river. Peg Leg's feathers became shiny again, and his emerald head glistened in the sun.

The usual number of ducks didn't come back from river trips, but Pete made it. I hunted a few times, but at a marsh far from our home. Then when the hunting season finally closed about the middle of November, one last string of blackbirds dipped low over the ponds, as if in salute, before heading south.

We put snow tires on the car, and sand in the back of Bumpy, and a red snow plow was mounted out front. And none too soon, because December was ushered in with a snow storm.

The Mill Pond froze, and then the smaller ponds with the springs got coatings of ice, and what ducks hadn't been killed or gone south were edging up into the open water of Watercress Creek.

Besides Peg Leg, there were four drakes and a single huge brown hen with a white ring around her neck. We couldn't guess what her breeding was, but suspected it was one of the wild-domestic crosses which were so often making an appearance.

"It'll probably pollute the wild flocks," Gwen said one day.

"What will pollute the wild flocks?" I asked.

"All those domestic strains that keep getting into the bloodlines of the wild ones."

"Don't worry about it," I said. "Most of the cross-breeds get shot because, unlike the truly wild ones, they are not wary enough to avoid the guns. Then, even if they are, that tiny bit of domestic blood that gets into the wild flocks is like a spit in the ocean. It doesn't change a thing."

Gwen laughed. "Well, when you put it like that."

A friend of mine, C. P. (Chappie) Fox, noted circus historian and the man who manages the circus museum at Baraboo, Wisconsin, (now in Florida with Ringling Brothers circuses) had once voiced the same objections to permitting domestic and wild ducks interbreeding. In fact, we had even argued about what might happen to the wild ones if permitted to indiscriminately cross with the tame ones.

Of course, it has been going on for years, and nobody has yet noticed any changes in the wild flocks. In fact, the domestic blood, if anything, might actually improve the wild stock. But, of course, nobody really knows.

Pete was wild and Gertie was tame. Their offspring, by now named Salt and Pepper, were more tame than wild, perhaps because they had been raised behind wire and by a domestic mother.

We thought about such things, and sometimes we talked about them during the supper hour at the kitchen table. And our lives were so full that we hardly

72

noticed that winter had gotten such a grip on Little Lakes as nobody, not even our octogenarian neighbor, Jerry Washicheck, Sr., could remember.

Between Christmas and New Year's, ice began to creep up Watercress Creek, something we'd never seen it do before. It stilled the sound of water running over the stones, edged out from the banks squeezing the little flock of ducks into tighter and tighter quarters.

Then one morning on my way to the post office I stopped the car at the bridge and watched. Peg Leg had been forced to join the four other drakes and the big hen. The six of them were squeezed into an opening in the ice which was hardly five feet across. All were paddling to keep ice from further encroaching on their last little watery domain.

The children were, of course, home enjoying Christmas vacation, and during the day they came often to watch the ice locked flock.

"What'll happen if the creek freezes solid?" Dianne asked that night at supper.

"I don't really know," I said, "but I expect they'll have to take to the air and look for open water. Probably fly down to Lake Michigan to wait the cold spell out."

"What will they eat out there?" Mary asked. "There's no food for them there. They can't dive for fish like the mergansers or for snails like the bluebills."

"Maybe they'll stop off at the Juneau Park Lagoon. The city keeps it aerated so it's always open, and there are always lots of ducks to decoy them down."

"Maybe they'll just sit until they freeze tight," Dianne said.

Well, she was right. It could happen. I'd seen it on

73

more than one occasion, and I'd rescued more than one duck, chopped it from the ice. Usually they were the foolish or the crippled.

"Maybe we ought to help," Mary said.

"Help with what?" Debbie asked.

"Help them keep a hole open."

So after supper, with two flashlights lighting the way, we walked down the long road to the bridge and the bright beams caught the ducks in their circles of light. Their pool of open water had been reduced to an area less than four feet across.

"You know what's strange?" Mary asked.

"What's strange?" I prompted her.

"They aren't fighting with Pete. They're leaving him alone."

Debbie explained it before I had a chance to. "Whenever there's trouble, big trouble that threatens everybody—like a flood or an earthquake—personal differences don't matter."

She was silent then, so I thought it was a good chance to get in a lick, a lesson on life: "That's right. Black, white, red, or yellow. Catholic, Protestant, or Jew. Rich or poor. It doesn't make any difference when some great calamity besets a people, a thing like war, for instance. Then everybody forgets their differences and pulls together."

Debbie snorted impatiently. I could see the twin puffs of steam come from her nostrils. She hadn't appreciated my elaboration. I suppose to her I was belaboring a cliché. So she said, "Well, let's just forget about all these lessons in life and get on with doing something for those ducks. It's twenty below zero in case anybody forgot."

"Maybe we could widen their hole by breaking up the ice," Dianne said.

"I don't know. I hate to frighten them into flight," I said, "because where would they go?"

"But what else?" Mary asked. "If we don't do something they're going to be frozen in solid by morning."

So Dianne and Debbie went back up the road to the garage for a crowbar, axe, and two shovels. Then we began breaking our way from shore out to where the ducks were imprisoned. All six ducks swam nervously as the axe and the shovels rang out on the crisp air.

Then without warning the four drakes jumped into the air and we saw them briefly in flight as our lights swung skyward. We could see they were headed in the direction of the frozen Mill Pond.

"Think they'll come back?" Mary asked.

"I don't know," I said.

"Well, let's finish the job," Debbie said.

So we proceeded, and then Peg Leg catapulted himself into the air, and the big female, who obviously couldn't fly, went slipping and sliding along the ice until she disappeared in the direction of Clear Pool and the Mill Pond.

"You know, I think we've done it," Dianne said.

All of us were wet by now, in spite of the fact that I was wearing waders, and the three girls had on boots. And where we had been sprayed by water, it froze so that our clothing crackled when we moved.

"Might as well finish," Debbie said.

And so we did, widened the hole until it stretched from bank to bank, and then hoping they would return, we went shivering to the house.

The children went down to the creek early the next

morning. Then on my way to the post office I stopped on the bridge. The hole was frozen shut. It was jagged with chunks of ice we had broken loose the night before.

After picking up the mail, I drove along the west shore of the Mill Pond. There was one duck standing on the ice, and it looked like the female who couldn't fly. Then I drove down to the Fox River, just to check if perhaps the current hadn't kept a sliver of river open. It was frozen solid.

That night everybody speculated on where the four ducks and Pete might have gone.

"Lake Michigan likely," I said. "Even if it's frozen for a mile or more out from shore, if they fly far enough, they're sure to find open water."

"Doesn't it ever freeze all the way over?" Mary asked.

"It did one year that I know of. It was back in the thirties. I was a cub reporter for the *Sheboygan Press*. I remember going out on an ice-breaking tug to rescue a fishing boat which was frozen in."

"Where would they go then, if it froze over?"

"Well, they could head south, of course, but likely they'd go to the Juneau Park Lagoon. Milwaukee keeps it open for just such emergencies."

We dropped the subject of the ducks. The children talked about what they'd like to do on New Year's Eve. Gwen wondered if we'd be doing anything.

"Not unless you want to go out," I said.

"I don't want to," she said. "Too many cars. Too many drinking drivers. I'd rather stay home."

"Think I'll stay home, too," Debbie said.

"We can watch 1968 come in on television. We can

see it come in at eleven o'clock in New York," Mary said. It intrigued them to think they could see the New Year arrive in New York an hour before it got around to arriving in Wisconsin.

But the next night, instead of watching 1968 come in on television, we were all in the car and headed for Milwaukee.

We had four high-powered flashlights and were going to the Juneau Park Lagoon on the lake front to see if Peg Leg was there.

"This is silly," Gwen said, as we zipped along the freeway.

"Sure is," I agreed. "In all my years I've spent some fantastically weird New Year's Eves—one even getting shot at in an airplane over Europe—but I can't say I ever spent a New Year's Eve looking for a duck."

It had all started at the supper table, so I suppose Pete had really been on their minds all along. Mary was first. "What if Pete is sitting on the ice somewhere or in a snowy field starving to death?" she said, and her eyes were shining with tears which wanted to spill and run down her cheeks.

"He's tough," Dianne said. "Don't worry about him."

"But what if he is?" Mary persisted.

"I'm sure he made the lake," I said, "or maybe he even stopped at the lagoon."

"I'd sleep better if I knew. I hardly slept at all last night," Mary went on.

"To tell you the truth, neither did I," Gwen said.

Then one by one they all broke down and expressed the concern they'd been feeling, and it wound up with me promising to take them to the Juneau Park Lagoon to see if Pete was among the ducks which wintered there.

It was freeway all the way until we got to the lake front. Then we followed Lake Shore Drive, and within a few minutes we were parked a couple of hundred feet from the lagoon.

Only Mary didn't have a flashlight, so she stayed with me. Then even before we came down to the shores of the lagoon, we could hear the subdued quacking, and sometimes a quick whirr of wings, as one or another duck lifted a little to fan the air.

When we turned on the lights, ducks tumbled from where they'd been resting on the hard-packed snow along the shore into the water. There were hundreds. Mostly mallards, and lots of drakes, all with shiny emerald heads, and almost all looking exactly like Peg Leg Pete.

There were other species, too. Widgeon, pintails, and a couple of hooded mergansers. There were a few American goldeneyes, one bufflehead, and a big blue goose swimming nervously in the bright cone of our lights.

We separated and each took a section of pond and began to study the great crowd of mallard drakes to see if one swam with stuttering, short, jerky, off-balance strokes.

Twice we all met back at the car, and twice we all went back to look again. Lake Shore Drive traffic began to increase. The New Year's Eve crowd was starting to converge on the supper clubs which dot Milwaukee's east side. Then a car stopped, and two flashlights approached.

"What's going on here?" a voice asked.

It was the police, and I heard Debbie whisper, "It's the fuzz."

For a moment I didn't know what to say. I suppose I was hesitant, perhaps I even stammered. But finally I got it out, "We're looking for a duck."

"For New Year's Day dinner?"

"No. You don't understand. It's a special duck."

"Oh, a special duck for New Year's Day dinner. Say, like a big, fat one?"

"It's our duck," Mary popped up.

"You got your name on it?"

"Well, not exactly," I said, "you see we cut his leg off."

"You hear that one, Bill? They mark their ducks by cutting their legs off."

"What I mean is," I tried to explain, "he was in a muskrat trap, and . . ."

"Oh, so you're setting muskrat traps to catch the ducks!"

"No!" I was angry, "we're not setting traps for the ducks."

"Don't you use that tone on me," the officer said, "or you'll spend New Year's Eve inside looking out through bars."

Debbie piped up: "Our duck got away. We thought he might be down here."

"Oh? Well, it's a good story, but I don't believe it. Last week a guy claimed he was a wildlife biologist studying the ducks. We found his sack in the bushes. It had five ducks, all with their necks wrung."

"It's the truth," I said.

"We wouldn't lie," Gwen said.

"I know. Nobody ever lies," the officer said. "Everybody tells the truth."

"Well, how can I prove it to you that we're not doing anything wrong?"

"Best way I can think of is by getting back in your car and getting out of here."

Slowly we filed back to the car. The officers walked behind us. I heard one say, "Maybe they're hungry."

The other one answered, "Well, they can get a Christmas basket at the Salvation Army just like anybody else."

On the way home, Gwen said to me, "Happy New Year, Mel."

And I said, "Yeah, honey, Happy New Year."

(10

Subsequently we went back during daylight hours to the Juneau Park Lagoon to see if we could spot Pete in the feathery armada. If he was there, we didn't find him.

The big female with the white ring around her neck disappeared from the ice of Mill Pond, and I suspect Mrs. Yug gave her shelter. She raised ducks, and she put corn down along the edge of the water for the wild ones.

Then Gertie died. Mary came in from doing chores one night after school and said, "Dad, there's something the matter with Gertie. I think she's dead."

"You *think* she's dead! Don't you know?"

"Well, her eyes are open, but she just sits there and doesn't move."

So I went out, and Gertie was indeed dead. Evidently her tired old heart had just not been able to pump anymore. She was squatting on the leaves in a corner she had taken for herself, and to look at her you'd swear she was alive, just resting there, content with her lot.

Her neck was folded back into a comfortable S, and

the tip of her bill came down and was resting on her ample bosom. Her eyes were open, and in the little light from the open door, they even gleamed. But when I picked her up, I could feel the rigidity—rigor mortis had already set in.

So we got her a cardboard box, lined it with leaves from the floor of the pen, and then put her in the back shed where there was already a black-and-white rabbit which had died since frost made the ground too hard for grave digging.

Strangely, as much as the children loved the old duck, there were no tears. But that's the way it was sometimes. They might cry their eyes out if a duck or a rabbit or some other pet died before its time. But if the animal or bird was old, and especially if it was weary (as Gertie had recently been), they looked upon death as a blessing.

As the days passed then, we talked less and less about Pete. We did make a few trips out to some spring holes in the Kettle Moraine State Forest to see if he might have landed in the open water of one of these, but gradually, though not forgotten, he was at least not uppermost in our minds.

Winter, if not a hard time at Little Lakes, is certainly always a busy time. The muskrat trapline had to be serviced, and what 'rats were caught had to be skinned and the pelts stretched. The lawn tractor, equipped with a small plow, had to come out after every fresh snow so Fish Pond might be cleared so plant life below might get enough light to manufacture oxygen for the bass and bluegills.

Once we had plowed the pond with Bumpy. Then one day, with Mary and Debbie in the cab with me and

Dianne watching from the shore, we hit a spring hole and went through. I had had to scramble while the truck was going down to shove the two children through a window. I had swallowed a little icy water before I managed to get clear.

So now we did the plowing with the little tractor, and since it cut but a three-foot swath, it was a considerable job to plow a couple of acres, especially if the snow was deep.

Then, of course, water containers for all the pets froze every day and every night. The children kept two sets of cans for each animal and bird. So while one set of containers was thawing out in the basement, the other set, containing fresh water, was available for drinking, until it in turn froze.

Of course, the water hole in Fish Pond had to be cleared of ice every morning and every evening so the horses could drink, the bedding for the dogs had to be changed often so they might stay warm. There were many bird feeders, and literally hundreds of birds—cardinals, bluejays, grosbeaks, chickadees, nuthatches, etc.—kept emptying them, so at least once a day someone had to make the rounds and fill them again.

Sidewalks had to be shoveled, roads and trails plowed, conifers which had been flattened by heavy, wet snow had to be lifted and shaken free of their burdens. And then, when there was time, there would be brush to haul to the burning pile when I'd cut a dead or dying tree with the chain saw for wood chunks to feed the two hungry fireplaces, one in the basement and the other upstairs in the living room.

Of course, we kept an eye open for Pete. As the weather moderated, the creek opened and most of

Clear Pool came free of ice. Other ducks visited, especially goldeneyes from Lake Michigan, but neither Pete nor any other mallards came back.

Little Lakes had, however, become a mecca for crowds of other wild animals and birds. It was the first year—1968—that snowmobiles really became a problem. It seemed there were hundreds roaring across the countryside, and of course, the Fox River with its flat, frozen marshes, was the ideal place for them to speed day and night with a minimum of interference from anything or anyone.

The Fox River, winding through its shallow valley, was a natural wintering place for wildlife. The wild ones came because the thick stands of rushes and reeds held off the snow and made ideal shelters. They came because there were mice and muskrats for the predators, and weed seeds of all kinds for the birds.

But the snowmobiles flattened the marshes, broke down the natural shelters which had been insulated by snow, and the roar of the engines frightened the inhabitants of the valley out onto the hillsides.

Most, however, really had no place to go. The slopes leading down to the river were intensively farmed. There was no cover. Woodlots were scarce, and even these were invaded by snowmobilers.

We made our feelings about snowmobiles known right at the start, so none invaded our acres. But whole colonies of wild animals and birds came. Foxes, raccoons, mink, opossums, weasels, and I believe even some mice made the trek and began tunneling under our snow down among the grass roots.

Birds came, too, and it was ordinary to see a big pheasant sitting high in a tiny bird feeder feasting on sunflower seeds, even though corn had been spread on the ground for it.

Of course, such an influx of wildlife into such a limited area as ours couldn't mean anything except trouble. The foxes became so bold they hunted during daylight hours. Then, not finding enough food, they came right out onto the village streets, and men, perhaps frightened they might be rabid, took to patrolling their blocks at night with guns. One fox chased a pet cat right off the street, and when Mrs. Marjorie Shaft opened the door to let the cat in, the fox almost got into the house too.

Coming home late at night we'd sometimes surprise a fox in the garage, and often during the day we might jump one from its nest, and send it scurrying for the thicker cover of the spruce groves.

So, perhaps Peg Leg wouldn't have survived. Maybe one of the foxes would have gotten him. Of course, we put out food of every description, but it never seemed to be enough. The place was just too crowded, and when wild animals and birds are too crowded they do strange things, and there was much fighting, especially around the feeders.

Gwen and I walked the river in the face of an icy wind one day just to see what was happening down there. The marshes were flattened, not only by snowmobiles, but by all-purpose terrain vehicles. The flattened snow froze hard, of course, and it was like walking on concrete. We went two miles upstream and never saw as much as one rabbit track.

It was a difficult situation. Many of the snowmobilers were our friends. We wondered if they couldn't see what they were doing, how their machines were upsetting not only the equilibrium of a once peaceful village, but also destroying the habitat of a beautiful countryside.

Sometimes, rather timorously I'm afraid, we suggested that the snowmobilers stay to marked trails and thus spare much of the natural wintering habitat. But generally it was like talking to a drug addict. They couldn't see how they were hurting anything, even themselves, and so like most who didn't like the snowmobiles, we generally suffered in silence, but sometimes we cursed, especially if at two or three in the morning we'd be awakened by the roar of a fleet of machines cruising up the frozen river valley.

We hoped spring would come early, but winter lingered. Finally, however, the snow became too slushy for any except the most foolhardy snowmobilers, and then gradually the concentration of wild ones at Little Lakes began to disperse.

What's more, ducks began to filter back from the south, and we went more often to the ponds to see if Peg Leg Pete might not be among them.

Geese filled the skyways, too, and we had a visit from Duke, a gander who had once made his home with us, and about whom I wrote the book *Wild Goose, Brother Goose*. When Duke's mate, Duchess, was killed by a dog, we had taken him, and his goslings, to the Horicon Marsh National Wildlife Refuge and turned him free among the tens of thousand of Canadas gathered there. But each spring he visited, sometimes for a day, sometimes for several days, and he always had another goose with him, and so we assumed, of course, that he had taken a new mate.

With the Mill Pond open, a lot of ducks always congregated just off Mrs. Yug's front lawn. We took binoculars to look across to see if Peg Leg was among them.

But it was Mrs. Yug herself who first spotted Pete. One morning at the post office, after saying good morning, she said, "You know that one-legged duck? He's down on the Mill Pond."

"You mean Peg Leg Pete?" I asked.

She laughed. "I guess so. Yes, Peg Leg Pete."

Villagers, of course, knew about Peg Leg because I had written about him in a Sunday nature column I did for the *Milwaukee Journal*.

Gwen was all smiles when I told her. "The children will sure be happy," she said. The children were, of course, at school, but when they came home in the afternoon they postponed chores to slosh through the marsh to Mrs. Yug's shoreline to see for themselves.

"Where do you think he was?" Mary asked at supper that night.

"Maybe he was down at Juneau Park all the time and we just missed him," Debbie said.

"Could be," I agreed.

"I think he went south," Dianne said.

"How far would he have had to go to find open water?" Gwen asked.

"Probably southern Illinois," I said.

"How far is that?" Mary asked.

"Oh, maybe three hundred miles. Maybe a little farther."

"Is that far? For a duck, I mean?" Mary asked.

"Not really. The way Pete could fly, he'd have no trouble making forty miles an hour. Figure it out. If he started that night when we frightened him out of the creek, he'd have been down there before daylight."

"Wow!" Dianne said.

"Yeah, wow!" I said.

"They sure can travel," Mary said.

"They sure can," I agreed.

"I still think he was probably sitting it out down at the lagoon," Debbie said.

Next day the children reported Peg Leg had flown over the duck pen a number of times craning his neck to look down.

"Do you suppose he's looking for Gertie?" Mary asked.

"I suppose so. I suppose he is," I said.

"Well, that's sad."

"Yes, it is sad," I agreed.

Next day southern Wisconsin was visited by a cold snap. The thermometer plunged to zero. All the ponds froze. The raft of ducks which had been on the Mill Pond disappeared.

Then on my way to the post office I parked on the bridge, and there upstream from me swam Peg Leg, four mallard drakes, and the big female duck with the white ring around her neck.

That night at the supper table I told the children, but they had already seen Pete and the rest of the flock on the creek.

"It's just as though winter never happened," Mary said.

"Yeah, they're all right back where they started," Dianne said.

"Ain't it a fact," I agreed.

(11

Many ducks visited during the northward migration in that spring of nineteen hundred and sixty-eight, but only a few pairs of teal stayed—except, of course, for Peg Leg and the four mallard drakes, and the big hen, who couldn't fly in any case.

Naturally, the drakes had begun making passes at the single hen. I think sometimes she must have gone out of her mind with all that attention, and we'd hear her quacking all the way up to the house, as she planed along the water, using her wings as oars, to stay out ahead of first one and then another of her emerald-headed suitors.

"They'll kill her," Dianne said one day. "Maybe we ought to take a landing net and catch her and pen her up."

"She probably loves it," I said. "Just leave her be. Eventually she'll settle it, and then the fighting will be over."

In the beginning Pete just sat off to one side as the other four drakes bickered among themselves. Sometimes he flew up to the pen on the hill and circled as though looking for Gertie. Not seeing her, he'd head back, skid to a halt on the water, and then swing over to his submerged rock, and perched on his one good leg, let his little orange stump dangle so just the tip of it was in the water.

Up in the pen the Pekin had been laying eggs for a month already. The children had been taking them from her and eating them for breakfast, because duck eggs are sweeter, or so at least they claimed.

"Aren't you going to let her have a brood?" I asked.

"We don't think so," Dianne said. "Just look at the ones from last year. They're not exactly what you'd call good looking ducks."

And they weren't. In some of the crosses, there had been improper wing development, and now a few had short, sparsely feathered flippers where strong wings should have been. A few had abnormally tiny heads which were almost pointed, and it seemed all were sterile, all "mules," because none showed any inclination to mate.

"Maybe you're right," I said. "Maybe it's best you pick up the eggs."

Salt and Pepper, the get of Gertie and Pete, were turned loose on the ponds, along with Aristotle and Plato. Salt and Pepper stayed away from the little flock on the creek, and neither showed any interest in finding a hen, so we assumed they too were either impotent or sterile.

It did not surprise us. We had seen it happen before —even in the fish world. Once we had crossed bluegills with green sunfish hoping to get a bigger, better-tasting fish. Thousands hatched, but most were stunted, and they could not reproduce.

The red-shouldered hawks, Teelon and Taalon, were a little late getting back, but they got busy right away adding sticks to the old nest in the dead elm, and they were ravenous. So we got on with shooting grackles for them, so the peace at Little Lakes would not be ruptured by raids on any of its other residents.

One pair of foxes stayed—a pair of grays. They had young somewhere in one of the spruce groves, and though we rarely saw them, they left ample signs about, though mostly they seemed content with mice caught in the clearings, and even in the vacant lots of a subdivision which was growing to the east of us.

Meanwhile, down on the creek, the battle for Beulah —new name the children had given the brown hen— continued. Then one day Pete got into it.

I was fishing for a meal of trout out of Clear Pool when suddenly with the speed and grace and unbelievable dexterity of a sparrow hawk, I saw Pete pursue one of the mallard drakes through, around and over the billowing willows which held in Clear Pool.

It was no contest. Pete drove the drake right out of the area and down to Mill Pond where he sat quacking indignantly.

In quick succession then, Pete routed the other three drakes in attacks which were nothing short of amazing. In pursuing them, he sometimes dove like a falcon, literally driving his adversary to the ground where there would be a flurry of wings and bills before the victim of his savagery could once more get off and away to the safety of Mill Pond.

By noon the four drakes had been driven from the creek, and I still hadn't caught enough fish for supper. Then while I quickly caught two more rainbows, Pete, seemingly none the worse for his wars, came swimming with Beulah by his side, out of the creek onto Clear Pool.

I couldn't help but feel elated. Many times (as with all of us) life has presented me with what at the time seemed insurmountable problems. Sometimes I had backed off, retreated, though I had all my faculties and was not missing a leg, or anything else. And here was Pete, whom I'd written off as a loser the day I'd amputated his leg, just knocking the props out from under my feeling of compassion for him.

I told the children about it at supper that night. They too were elated. (So I hoped Pete's example might fortify them against any dark and desperate days which might lie ahead.)

"Just goes to prove," I said, "what can be done if you put your mind to it."

"We get the point," Debbie said. "You don't have to elucidate."

Sometimes I got angry underneath when Debbie stuck her little barbs into my philosophizing, but I knew it was only part of growing up. Still, I intended capsulizing lessons in living, if only for the benefit of the now nine-year-old.

Of course, now that I think of it, I imagine even Mary got the point without any help from me. Children today are mentally far and away out ahead of the children I grew up with.

Life, of course, was burgeoning around us. It was July of nineteen hundred and sixty-eight. New life crowded Little Lakes. Tens of thousands of pale young fish skittered like wind across the water as bigger bass rose to attack. The warm shallows were pimply with frogs, and

a wing shadow sent shivers through schools of pol-
lywogs yet waiting to rid themselves of their tails and
to grow legs.

Insects hatching turned flat water into a rain of a
hundred rings as they rose, and in the stagnant shallows
of the marsh, mosquitoes paused briefly at the surface
to dry their delicate wings before joining the whining
cloud above.

A million insects? Ten million maybe. A swallow
could glut itself in one glide, and a stilted heron might
get all the fish fry it could hold in ten cautious steps.

Along the dikes, canary grass grew head high.
Beyond the pasture fence, where the horses couldn't
stretch their necks, clover was white and purple.

Now there was no stifling life. A root would split a
rock to put tendrils up to leaf in the sun. Blessed by
frequent rains, the earth responded generously and
Little Lakes became a riot of mid-summer blooms—
brazen flowers of red, bright blue—all the vivid colors
which spring can never quite manage.

Nests were full to overflowing with birds, and nests
of rabbits spewed youngsters out across the lawn.
Young gray squirrels played endless hours in the sun,
and woodchucks, not much larger than baseballs, came
up occasionally to look at the sky.

The hawks had three eggs in their nest. We had
climbed an adjacent tree to look down with binoculars,
and in fact, a friend had been contemplating putting a
platform up and covering it with canvas so he might
photograph the birth, feeding, and growth of Teelon's
and Taalon's offspring.

Members of bird clubs came from Milwaukee to marvel, though we discouraged such miniature safaris be-

cause of what crowds did to the even tenor of the wild ones' ways—not to mention what it did to our writing schedule.

Then one night at supper, with all of us pleasantly hungry after a full day, Gwen, who always sat so she could look out through a sun-room window, suddenly said, "The big elm! It's gone!"

It sounded silly, her saying something like that. It was a calm, peaceful evening. The sun was still shining. There was no wind. The elm gone? Down? So what could have happened to make a gigantic elm suddenly disappear?

When no one said anything, she repeated, "I tell you, it's gone!"

Only then did we get up and go out onto the sun porch, and I'll never know why we didn't hear the crash unless it was because of the radio, but there the big elm lay, partly among the surrounding cedars, but with its splintered crest out on the lawn. Pieces had been catapaulted nearly up to the house, a distance of almost two hundred yards.

The hawks were circling, and we forgot about supper. The tree had taken out four electric lines which went to Clear Pool and the one-room cabin which stood on its shores. It had taken out about twenty cedars about eighteen feet tall. It had driven limbs so far into the soft soil that we never did get them out, and had to eventually settle for only cutting them off at ground level.

"What in the world made that happen?" I asked Gwen. But she had no answer. She was watching the circling hawks.

Then while the kids went in among the thick cedars

94

to see if they could find the remains of the nest, I went to the trunk to see what had made the tree fall. When I came back out I had the answer.

"Osmosis," I said to Gwen.

"Osmosis?"

"That tree was so punky it acted like a sponge. It was sucking up water from Fish Pond until it was saturated. Finally, I suppose, the last solid fiber became pulpy and down she came."

We both went in to look. We picked up chunks of wood and when we squeezed them, the water ran as out of a wet dish rag.

Back where the trunk lay among the thicker cedars, we could hear the kids. "All wrecked. All broken." It was Mary.

"What'll the hawks do?" Gwen asked.

"Probably start somewhere else. Build a new nest."

"Must be hard on them," she said.

"Not so hard as you might think. They're programmed to accept tragedy. That's where they got it over us. We're not." After I'd said it, I was glad Debbie wasn't close enough to hear, because I'm sure she'd have had some little caustic, if harmless remark to make.

We went back to the house, but we didn't eat much. Next day I took off from my routine of writing and, with a chain saw, went down to begin cleaning up.

Within a few days the hawks started building in the top of one of the weeping willows which billowed out over Blue Pool.

"That's a foolish place to build," I said.

"Why?" Gwen asked.

"Too much traffic. It's right above the diving board. They'll never get any peace."

And that's the way it was. The children were out of school, and when they weren't working, Blue Pool was their favorite place. Still the hawks continued building. Then one night, just before dark, we heard a shot from across the Mill Pond. In the morning Taalon was missing, and only the big female was carrying sticks to the nest.

We never did find Taalon's body, but we were sure someone had shot him. Sporadically then, all that summer, Teelon worked on the nest, and she even came back next spring to carry more sticks. Eventually then, along about the start of the summer of nineteen hundred and sixty-nine, she disappeared and we never saw her again.

But to get back to nineteen hundred and sixty-eight. The big, brown duck, Beulah, was nowhere around, but we saw Pete from time to time, so we assumed she had a nest somewhere. Of course, what we were anxiously waiting for was her reappearance with a clutch of ducklings in tow.

Sometimes we found the teal nests. It was easier to locate nests of those capable of flight. We'd watch their flights for water and then back, and get a pretty good idea of where the nest was hidden. With a walker like Beulah, she'd just disappear in the long grass and you might look for weeks and sometimes, perhaps, even be standing within a few feet of where she was sitting and never see her, such was her camouflage.

But the time came and went for the hen's reemergence, but no Beulah.

Meanwhile we kept busy. I had my writing. Debbie

was helping a neighboring school teacher with house and yard work. Dianne and Mary had the task of keeping a couple of acres of lawn mowed and helping Gwen with her flowers.

The flowers were all wild ones. As freeways went in, we scurried out ahead of the bulldozers digging up wild flowers and loading them into Bumpy (who had been derricked, none the worse for the wetting, out of the pond) for planting at Little Lakes.

Transplanting can sometimes be something of a shock, so Gwen kept other vegetation from crowding the immigrants, and she kept the soil loose and hauled water. Some survived, some didn't. But gradually over the years she was getting pockets of trillium, bellwort, Jacob's ladder, six or eight kinds of violets, jack-in-the-pulpits, May apples, hepatica, day lilys, shooting stars, adder's tongue . . . maybe fifty or more different kinds.

Then, of course, there were shrubs—wild grape, bittersweet, dogwood, multiflora rose, elderberry—almost a score or maybe more of seed- and berry-bearing plants calculated to keep the birds happy.

So we were all so busy that Beulah had been missing for almost two months before it dawned on us that she probably wasn't coming back, that something—disease or a fox or a dog or a man—had probably caught her while nesting, and that now her life was over.

Of course, we never knew. Sometimes an animal or bird disappeared and would turn up again months or even years later. Rickey, a raccoon, who had been our pet, was gone nearly two years before he came back emaciated, dragging a trap, and so cruelly injured I had no choice except to shoot him.

Some of the seagulls we'd raised—Sail and Soar, Swirl

and Swoop—having gained their wings went to Lake Michigan, and then intermittently visited us.

Woodchucks turned loose would come back, and one which had been a pet, grazes to this day evenings and mornings on the front lawn, and then hibernates in a deep burrow beneath the shed where the bodies wait for spring burial.

There have been crows, a tame bluejay, squirrels and Copperking, a pheasant cock, who had all remained half-tame, half-wild after being given their freedom.

We had never tried to hang onto any of the wild ones. Usually they became our wards for a time because they needed help. Soon as they could forage, they were given gradual freedom, a time of being intermittently cared for while adjusting to the life which better fitted their wild spirits.

So the disappearance of Beulah, though we regretted it, especially since she belonged to Pete, was not an occurrence of tragic proportions.

Still we always watched for her—even to this day—and Gwen would watch with me sometimes, especially evenings. Then, standing on the edge of the marsh, we would see Pete, up on his one good leg sound asleep on a log, and Gwen would say something like, "Do you think he dreams? And what do you think he dreams about?"

And I would tell her I thought all animals dreamed, but that their dreams were only concerned with the fabric of their daily lives. Then one night, when we were side by side in bed, she asked, "Mel, granted that there are many things which distinguish man from the animals, what one thing do you think stands out—makes them most different."

I had to think awhile, but then I said something like this: "The thing which most distinguishes man from the animals is probably man's capacity to wonder and to admire and to therefore feel humbly grateful in the presence of an awsome creation of nature."

"How do you mean?" she asked.

"Well," I said, "we—you and I—may come out on a starlit night and gaze in rapture at the heavens. But the owl does not look up. He looks only down for the mouse.

"We—you and I—may watch a sunset which expands our minds, but for the bird it is only a signal to find a night camp.

"We—you and I—can shiver at the brilliance of a river strewn with sun diamonds. But to the kingfisher it is only an annoyance, because the brilliance hides the minnow."

For a long time then we lay quietly beneath the blanket, almost touching, but not quite. From somewhere beyond the window we heard the muffled thunder of a night hawk's wings.

Then Gwen said, "For once I can't quite agree with you."

"How's that?" I asked.

"To me the capacity for concern most distinguishes man from animals. The virtue of compassion."

"Could be," I said.

And then she touched me, and I moved closer, and it was enough. We slept.

(12

Summer slipped slowly and almost softly into autumn. Debbie, done with high school, went to the University of Wisconsin—Milwaukee, but managed to get home weekends. Dianne and Mary endured the classroom, but shoes came off long before they got home. Trees began getting ready for winter, and their leaves turned many colors in a final celebration.

Peg Leg and a motley gang of wild and crossbred ducks were scattered across the eight ponds. They made regular flights to the Fox River, and I expect as far away as a big lake, Muskego, four miles to the east.

Teelon still hung around, but she had long given up adding sticks to the nest and only sat in the highest trees, her feathers so ruffed she gave the appearance of being disconsolate

The martins had left in August, and now the blackbirds were flocked and the tree swallows had gone to marshy staging areas where they swarmed like thousands of sun-kissed green bees. We heard the screech owls at night, and sometimes we went outside if there was a moon to see if migrating flocks were putting occasional shadows across its white face.

Then came the week when the duck hunting season was scheduled to open, and Gwen asked me if I were going hunting.

"I don't even have a license," I said.

"Well, that won't take but a few minutes."

"I don't know," I said. "I don't much feel like it."

"It might do you good. You work so hard. You're at the typewriter day and night. You don't go anywhere anymore. Why don't you hunt this season?"

She knew, of course, that hunting had once been a passion with me. She must have known also that I missed the thrill of coming to a frosty glade and seeing a buck bound away among the saplings, of crouching among the fragrant marshes along a lake front where the canvasbacks came catapaulting past at speeds of sixty miles per hour, of bucking hazel brush to put a ruffed grouse into such flight as sounded like muffled thunder.

We had been sitting at the kitchen table, and now I got up and went out into the sun-room where my guns stood in a rack.

They were dusty. I had hunted only a few times last fall and hadn't touched them since. I picked up the high-powered rifle, a .308 caliber with a four-power telescopic lens, and worked the bolt. It snapped in and out with the bright, sharp click of precision such as you'd expect from a well-built machine. I put it back and picked up a .28-gauge shotgun and threw it to my shoulder. It came up smoothly, as though it were an extension of me, like an arm.

"How's it feel?" Gwen asked, looking out through the kitchen door.

"Smooth. They feel all right. They feel good. Like old friends."

"Well, run on down to the Sportsman's Shack in Muskego and get a license."

"I'll need a duck stamp, too."

"Get it when you go to the post office tomorrow."

That night at supper I announced to Dianne and Mary that I was going duck hunting. For a moment there was silence, and I took it for disapproval. "You'd like a nice meal of wild ducks, wouldn't you?" I asked.

Mary, who is always hungry, went through the exaggerated motions of smacking her lips. "Would I? You bet!"

"When does the season open?" Dianne asked.

"Saturday noon."

"Where would you hunt?" Mary asked.

"The river, probably."

"It'll be crowded," Dianne said.

"What place isn't these days?" I said.

Everybody was quiet for a while then, and I wondered what was going through their minds. Years ago, of course, our two freezers had always been full of game. There had been deer from Wisconsin, moose from Ontario, quail from Florida, pheasants from South Dakota, sharptail grouse from Saskatchewan, ruffed grouse from many states, and cottontails which I then preferred to shoot with a bow and arrow.

Mary, of course, couldn't remember those days, and Dianne hadn't yet come to live at Little Lakes because I hadn't met and married her mother.

Of course, intermittently over the past eight or ten

years, I'd hunted. But if I went out four or five times a season it was a lot, and usually we never had more than one or two meals of duck, and sometimes a brace of pheasants.

We had sold one of the freezers, and then when the other malfunctioned, we hauled it out to the stable because it held five hundred pounds of oats on one side, and a hundred pounds of corn on the other and was verminproof.

There had been a time too, which both could remember, when I sometimes cropped surplus cottontails from our place by trailing them in the snow to where they crouched in their forms, and then shot them through the head with a pellet gun.

The rabbit shooting on our acres all but ended the year I shot Old Cripple. We rarely got a look at Old Cripple, whom we got to call Old Crip, but we knew a lot about him. After every fresh snow there'd be his tracks among the welter of cottontail tracks, one leg dragging to leave a groove in the snow the way a muskrat does when it drags its tail on an overland trek.

Occasionally we'd see Old Crip. He could run fairly fast for having what the children called an "unhinged" hind leg. But usually he spent his daytimes in such protected places as beneath a shed floor, down an old woodchuck hole, or safe in the heart of some rock pile.

Then one day after it had snowed most of the night, I decided it was time for a hasenpfeffer supper. Both children—Dianne and Mary—trailed along to watch, and that's the day I drilled Old Crip.

I had been tracking another rabbit, and a hundred times more than the kill, I enjoyed moving along the cottontail's trail. I have a theory, even about rabbits, and it is that perhaps we should not be so quick to write off their seeming acumen as pure instinct. I think, though I know many will not agree with me, that if a Little Lakes' cottontail lives through a winter's night and finds enough to eat to sustain life for one more day, perhaps there is at work a mind of sorts, something a little beyond a species' inherited reflex for action.

Granting (if I may digress for a moment) that most rabbit actions are the mere flexing of sinews as have been fashioned by countless generations of cottontails fleeing down whatever trails were necessary for survival, it would still appear they are gifted with a wild sort of fortitude which sometimes calls for personal and individual invention necessary to fit the circumstance.

For example, the rabbit I was tracking on the day I killed Old Crip, remembered to stay in the brambles because it knew that there no owl could penetrate. But then it left the brambles and made a long leap to a shelf of spruce shadow, and then followed under the protection of this evergreen skirt to the sunken garden where, it must have remembered, that during more prosperous times were all manner of tender, growing things.

But, of course, now, in this winter there was nothing except the snow streaking like white needles, so the rabbit's tracks move on to jump a wall and then to dare to come into the open under the bird feeders.

The birds having been thrifty, there was little to eat; and so I follow the tracks to where last winter it probably found the white mulberry sapling. But now the white mulberry had been protected by wire, and so the tracks went to where the wild rose is a barbed hedge, and here the tracks indicate it sat, perhaps even disappointed, because the succulent rose hips were covered with snow.

Back swiftly then, but never going so close to the doghouse as to cause an uproar, it found the sidewalk and tongued at the sprinkle of salt—a dark, moist place where the ice had had to be melted.

Down the steps alongside the house the tracks went to where the squirrel feeder usually offered corn. But snow had covered the corn. Then, as I tracked, in my mind's eye I could see the rabbit contemplating the vast, open space of snow swept lawn. It was almost as though, looking down at the tracks in the snow, I could see the rabbit lifting a little to move its ears in all directions for any sounds of danger. Then, perhaps thinking the owl would not risk this wind, the cottontail raced down a drifted trail where the plow had cut, and came safely beneath the crowded cones of young, bronze cedars.

I could see, from the track, that it nibbled a box elder seedling, but the seedling had been gnawed so many times the bark had toughened into a bitter scab.

So there was nothing except to risk danger again by racing across the snow covered Fish Pond. The tracks were far apart then, and only when the rabbit was among the brush willows did it rest. Then it cut a twig with its sharp teeth at precisely the place where next spring's catkin waited. The green morsel the rabbit got was hardly larger than the head of a pin, but by being industrious it got countless smidgins of green, and at last full, moved off into deep marsh grass.

By now, the children trailing behind me, were a little impatient. But then suddenly, off to one side of the trail, crouched like a fur muff in a form of dry grass, I saw what I assumed was the cottontail I was tracking. But it wasn't! And there was no way of knowing it was Old Crip. So I shot, and the rabbit ran a dozen feet before collapsing. The children shouted, "It's Old Crip!"

But it was too late. Old Crip was dead. The rabbit we had been tracking jumped out of a hiding place beneath a tiny spruce as we knelt to examine the body of Old Crip, but we had lost enthusiasm for the hunt.

Of course, no one would eat Old Crip though I'm sure he would have made as savory a hasenpfeffer as any of the other cottontails at Little Lakes. Instead, we put Old Crip's body, along with other frozen bodies in the back shed, to await burial in spring.

So sometimes when I think to hunt again, I remember the body of Old Crip in the shed, but mostly I remember how the children, though never shedding a tear or even uttering a single syllable of dismay, will honor this rabbit with a spring flower on a grave only because (I assume) life handicapped him with a crippled leg, and yet he faced the winter of his death and the winter of his life (they assume) undismayed.

So if my desire to hunt was still a thing to be reckoned with, I was gradually losing, if not the appetite for it, then the cold, calculating instinct which makes for a really good hunter as opposed to somebody who just goes out to shoot.

After my announcement that I was going duck hunting, we ate for a while in silence, and then Dianne asked, "Which of the dogs are you going to take?"

It was a silly question, but she had a love affair going with Brig, the German shorthaired pointer, and wanted him to get in on everything. But Brig was gun shy, and Eekim, the Chesapeake Bay retriever, was soft as a piece of cream cheese and made only for hugging, so that left Black Buck, a Labrador, who had been regularly retrieving the grackles I'd shot for the hawks.

So I said, "Well, Buck, of course."

"But Buck hasn't retrieved any ducks, has he?" Dianne asked.

I tried to think. "Yes, one teal. Two years ago. But he's picked up a couple of pheasants, and then Orin Benson has shot a number of pigeons over him."

(Orin Benson, a friend who lives in the heart of the Kettle Moraine Forest west about fifteen miles, is probably one of the finest dog trainers in the country. As a hobby, he and his wife, Lucille, raise timber wolves— one of which I have written about in a book titled *Flight of the White Wolf.*)

Mary looked up from her plate now, her brown eyes wide. "Couldn't we go along?" she asked.

"I don't know. Would you want to?"

I had seen her helping worms off a sidewalk so they wouldn't die in the hot sun, so I sometimes wondered how she felt about killing unnecessarily.

"I'd like to go," Dianne said.

"Me too," Mary said, eagerly.

So about nine o'clock on Saturday morning, along with Buck, we all crowded into Bumpy. In back we had a duck skiff, and in the boat was a bag of wooden decoys and a small, three-horsepower outboard motor.

We drove through town, down a beautiful country lane, and after a mile turned on the River Road. There were only two cars parked at the bridge when I eased Bumpy to a halt on the gravel shoulder.

As we skidded the skiff off the truck and down the

steep bank to the water, Dianne said, "It's going to be crowded."

"Oh, we'll have room," I said.

"I didn't mean in the boat," she explained, "I meant along the river."

She was right, of course, because that is the way it always is these days. And I suppose that's what makes it seem more like a circus than a hunt. Once, long ago, hunting was a private almost religious sacrifice. Now, especially if on public lands, it is like open warfare, and men are often bereft of the last shreds of civilized demeanor in their greed to get game.

I thought of that, and I thought of Debbie, and I wondered if, in her too conscious efforts to appear worldly and cynical she might not have some appropriate way of including even me in the ranks of the overly aroused gunners.

We got the skiff in, and when we were all in it, and after everything was loaded, we were well down in the water. I started the motor, and running at half-throttle, pointed the bow upstream. I always hunt upstream. Then if the motor quits, you always have the current to help you get back to where the truck stands.

It was a hot day for October, and I shucked my shirt and sat at the tiller in the stern stripped to the waist. The two girls sat together on the middle seat, and Buck was immediately in front of them in the bow.

I didn't know where I was going to hunt, but decided that the farther I got away from the bridge, the less chance there would be of running into other hunters.

We hadn't been afloat more than a few minutes, however, when we ran aground. It had been a dry summer.

The little river was low, and so there we sat on a mud flat.

I tried prying the boat free with an oar, but it wouldn't budge. "I think you two will have to go over the side to lighten the load," I said.

The girls liked the idea. The river was cool and they were sweating. But even after they were out, standing knee-deep in mud, the boat wouldn't budge.

"Maybe we can pull it," Dianne said.

The two girls bent to the task. Both, if not big, were strong. Dianne weighed perhaps one hundred and ten pounds, but I'd often seen her wrestle a hundred pound sack of oats around. Mary weighed more like seventy pounds, but she could walk away with a fifty pound sack of dog food on one shoulder.

So, after a few grunts for my benefit, they had the skiff moving. I helped with an oar, and then the water deepened. They got back in and I started the motor.

All along the shore, sometimes less than a gun-shot apart, hunters ranged awaiting the zero hour—the noon opening. It was silly and it was sad. They stood, many of them, in new, heavy hunting clothes, in cumbersome, shiny boots, an army looking to kill a duck, an anxious crowd of gunners waiting as if in line for their chance at shooting gallery targets.

We hadn't gone more than two hundred yards and once again we were stuck on a mud flat. The men and the boys on the shore laughed. Again the girls got out. And so it went. Me, sitting high and dry in the boat, looking like some king being dragged upriver by a pair of slaves.

Buck, too, acted important. He climbed on the middle seat and sat at strict attention, and the girls giggled as they wallowed through the mud dragging the both of us over one mud flat after another.

It wasn't long, of course, and both girls were covered with mud. I couldn't help laughing. To my laughter Dianne took exception. After all, she was a junior in high school, and if wallowing in the mud was still fun, she was an emerging lady and didn't appreciate being reminded how at heart she was still really a child. Then there were the other hunters, and that didn't help her sense of propriety.

So I stopped laughing, and I said, "We'll stop soon. First decent widening after a turn."

After the next curve in the river there was a wide place, and so we put into shore. I got out and we dragged the skiff to where we could hide it in the cattails. Then the girls took the wooden decoys and with the dog jumping and barking with delight, they placed the stools so as to represent a flock of feeding ducks.

They washed off then, and came back to where I was comfortably hidden behind the boat, and the thermos of Kool-Aid and the cookies came out, and after loading my gun, we settled down to wait.

It was nearly eleven-thirty. Shooting would start at noon. From time to time teal whisked up the river, but none accepted the invitation of our frauds to tarry.

Two men appeared on the opposite bank of the river, and when they saw our decoys, moved upstream. We could hear voices behind and below us, so we knew there were many hunters about.

At ten minutes to twelve, somebody jumped the gun and the shooting started. We saw no ducks. Then at noon there were a few flocks extremely high, headed south.

"Bad day," I said. "Should be cold, windy."

"There! There!" Dianne whispered.

I was lighting my pipe. I dropped it. But before I could get my gun up, the duck was out of range. It was a wood drake, resplendent as all the colors of the rainbow melted together to make a bird.

"I'm glad you didn't see it in time," Mary said.

I was glad, too.

Intermittently we heard shots, and sometimes we saw ducks in the distance, and there were always voices, but no bird came within range. Once there were two hawks sailing, and Dianne said she hoped they'd stay high so nobody would shoot them, and once a bittern flew by, but it dumped right down in the tall grass, maybe figuring that was the safest place to be.

The afternoon began to drag, and I was on the verge of calling an end to the hunt, when Dianne said, "Look. Look. Over there!"

I raised my head, and there, a couple of gun ranges downstream were four mallards busily bottom feeding, oblivious of the fact that all across Wisconsin that afternoon thousands upon thousands of hunters were looking for them or their cousins.

"Where'd they come from?" I asked.

"I don't know," Dianne said.

"They couldn't have flown in. We'd have seen them," I explained.

"How else?" Mary asked.

"That little creek over there," I pointed. "They must have come down that creek."

111

"Well, aren't you going to shoot them?" Dianne asked.

"They're too far away."

"Can't you sneak up on them?"

"I'll try," I said. "Hold the dog so he doesn't follow and scare them off."

I was off then, like I'd been taught to crawl in basic training, across the boggy land, through the rushes and reeds, panting and puffing.

When I thought I was close enough to risk a look, I raised my head. There were two hens and two drakes. One of the drakes stayed a considerable distance from the other three as if he didn't belong. I thought to crawl a little closer, and then Buck, having jerked free from the girls, came bounding through the grass.

A hen sounded the alarm, and the four leaped from the water. I was on my knees shooting. Both hens came down on the first shot. I got the drake which had been with them on the second. Then the lone drake swung back, as if to look down on the three which had returned to the river surface, and I trained my gun on him.

In the instance before I pulled the trigger I noticed something peculiar about the drake. And in the next instant I saw the stump, the little stub without a foot.

It was Peg Leg Pete!

I knelt there like a statue, my gun still aimed skyward, while Pete flew well out of range.

I can't remember exactly all which followed or the things that were said. But it went something like this:

"That was Pete!" Dianne almost screamed.

"I know," I shouted back at her.

"Did you hit him?" Mary asked.

112

"No. Almost. But I saw in time."

I'm sure there was much more, but that was the gist of it, and of course, our afternoon of hunting was over. We picked up the decoys, the three dead ducks, and the kids hauled me and the dog back to the bridge.

When we landed, Robert Greene, my friend the game warden, was there.

"How'd you do?" he asked.

"Got three."

Then he saw them. "Say those are big, fat mallards. Man, they sure look as though they've been corn fed."

"Don't they though," I said.

And though the children had been a part of the misadventure, now they looked at me with accusing eyes. Or maybe I only imagined that they did, because we were almost positive the three were a part of the home flock we had often fed.

Bob helped us load the boat. Then as we were driving away, he said, "You're lucky. Most guys I've talked to never got a shot. Some never saw a duck."

In the cab of the truck it was quiet, except for the sound of the dog panting in the heat.

(13

Though no one spoke all the way home from our hunt, I'm sure we were all thinking the same thing. So when I came down the drive I stopped Bumpy on the bridge and we separated, going to various places Peg Leg might be if he'd successfully run the gauntlet of guns and made it home.

When we reassembled on the bridge no one could report having seen the drake. "There's a half-dozen ducks on the Mill Pond," Dianne said, "but Pete wasn't with them." Mary reported seeing Salt and Pepper, Gertie's offspring, but Pete obviously hadn't come back.

"Well, it doesn't mean he's dead," I said. "There are dozens of sloughs or potholes without hunters where he might have dropped in to wait until dark."

We all knew that could be the case, but we also had terrible visions of Pete's limp body being stuffed into someone's hunting coat. We could see Pete's bright feathers being plucked and scattered to the wind, and his round, little body being eviscerated and made ready to receive sage dressing or an apple or an onion.

We plucked the ducks. It was a painful experience. Supper was a wake. Finally Gwen said, "Just what is wrong. I should think you'd all be happy. You got three nice ducks, more than enough for a big meal."

So I told her how I'd almost shot Pete, and I told her how far from home he'd been, and I told her how many hunters had been stationed along the river banks. "And we think," I added, "the three we got were ones we've been feeding."

Then she was silent, too, and all that night the house was like a morgue, because the children didn't turn on television but went to their room, and because Gwen didn't have the sewing machine going, but sat with a book in her lap looking out where the yard light illuminated the blue spruce.

Finally at nine-thirty, when it was time for Mary to go to bed, the girls came downstairs, and Dianne said, "Maybe we could go down and see if he's back."

"There's a lot of territory to cover down there," I said. "We could easily miss him."

"But it wouldn't hurt to look," Mary said.

I was for it, of course, but I suppose I didn't want to add to the girls' disappointment. If they didn't find him, it would only compound their sorrow.

"Please," Mary pleaded.

"Okay."

So we got the powerful flashlights, and I asked Gwen if she wanted to go along, but she said no, that she would pop some corn and make some chocolate so the children would have a treat before going to bed.

Our electric torches put white sidewalks of light down the length of the front lawn, and we got a glimpse of a mouse-hunting fox as it scooted for the cover of the spruce.

Even before we got to the shores of the Mill Pond we could hear the gabble of ducks. They obviously had heard us and seen the lights and perhaps even resented this intrusion into their nighttime of relative peace.

All three lights were brought to focus then on the flock which was loosely bunched where Watercress Creek lost its identity to the pond, and we began to sort them out. There was Salt and Pepper off to one side. There was a pintail drake, obviously wounded. There were two bluewing teal, swimming nervously and looking like miniatures of their larger cousins. There was a lesser Canada goose, over on the far shore, and I was sure he was carrying shot somewhere in his body, else he'd never have been on the pond, away from his flock. There was a spoonbill drake, and there were two mallard drakes, but we knew immediately that neither of them was Pete.

"Let's try Clear Pool," I said. So we came out of the waist-high spruce in which we'd been standing, and went beneath the arching willows, past the bathhouse, to the trail along New Pool. We never bothered to check New Pool. Besides being small, it dropped off precipitously and was no place for ducks.

Once a shadow whisked like a ghostly gesture across the beams of lights, and we stopped in our tracks.

"It's an owl," I said. "The one that lives in the wood duck house."

We had a metal house which a firm in Minnesota manufactured. It was painted olive drab, and fastened to a post for wood ducks, but instead a little owl always used it. He (or she) was an untidy housekeeper, and

116

when we'd clean it in springtime there would be bones and fur and the feathers of cardinals, bluejays and other birds—not counting the pellets of indigestible hair it regurgitated.

Then, because our minds were on Pete, we almost ran into the white-faced hornets' nest, which was a globular gray house of wasp paper hanging on the low branch of a spruce. We put the lights on the miracle of insect ingenuity, and there were three hornets crawling around the tiny entrance at the tip.

Standing there, with all three lights focused on the paper house, Dianne said, "They'd never find us in the dark."

"They might," I said. "I read somewhere they locate targets by the temperature of the target or by smell. I forget which."

"You're thinking of mosquitos," Mary said. "I read it in my science magazine."

"Maybe you're right, but I'm not going to find out," I agreed.

"Me either," said Dianne, and I'm sure she was thinking of a cousin who a few months previously had blundered into the nest and came away with enough warts to make a pickle envious.

So we went the long way around, and coming to Clear Pool scanned it with our beams of light, and then crossing the bridge above the dam, went down into the marsh.

Here water from Clear Pool cascaded a few feet and it drowned out other sounds. Below the dam the creek widened and water seeped off into a marsh of cattails and muskrat houses.

"He could be hiding in there," I said, "and of course we'd look forever and never find him."

We went anyway, as far as there was high ground, and then we stopped because beyond was a morass which seemed virtually impossible to negotiate. Standing in a line we poked into the dark corners of the marsh with our sharp shafts of light, and then Dianne's beam stopped on a muskrat house.

"There! There!" she said. All beams converged on hers, and in the brilliance, far more illuminating than even rays of the sun, sat a mallard drake.

"Is it him?" Mary asked.

"Sure looks like him," Dianne said.

"I don't know. I don't know," I said, leaning forward, as though that might help.

"I think it is," Mary said.

"Well, if it is, he's sick," Dianne said.

And indeed, the duck caught in the bright spot of the three lights, did look sick. Instead of standing erect, with head alert, ready to spring into flight, the drake lay flat, his head thrust out resting on the soggy moss.

"I'm going out there," Dianne said, starting forward.

"No, wait," I said, taking her arm. "It might be over your head. And you can't swim in that stuff. You'd just go right down."

"Maybe we could drag a boat over," Mary said.

I thought about it. "Too long a haul. All the way from Fish Pond? Through the spruce? It'd kill us to get a boat in here."

"Well, I'm going to try to get out there," Dianne said, starting forward again. Once more I took her arm.

"I'll go," I said. "Go back to the brush pile on the

118

other side of the bridge and get me a long, tough length of willow."

When I had the branch which was thick around as my wrist and perhaps ten feet long, I stepped off the solid ground and immediately went to my knees in the muck. It was cold, icy in fact, because the marsh was one vast welter of springs which in winter often put up bubbles of water which looked like miniature volcanos in the field of white snow.

I took five steps and went down so the water was up to my waist. "I don't know," I said, resting. "I don't know if I can get there. The mud is so deep."

The children said nothing, so I pressed forward, pulling one foot out of the muck, pressuring it forward, and sinking one step closer to the muskrat house.

I moved so slowly I made no sound. Even above the water going over the dam we heard a door slam somewhere up in the village, and then a car started. We heard the engine, and then the hum of rubber meeting the road.

When I was halfway to the muskrat house a lone blackbird, startled from its night camp, went away in a whirr of wings.

The water didn't get deeper, and I was thankful for that. The children turned off their lights. I rested often, turning off the light when I did, and then we were separated by the darkness as if we lived on different planets.

But I was going to make it, I was sure, though I didn't even know if the drake was Pete. But anyway, it was a pretty sick duck, and if I could end its suffering the children might think that Whoever was keeping score would put one more little check mark for me on the credit side of life's ledger.

But I didn't get the duck. When I was only a couple feet away and about to reach out, the drake slid off the 'rat house, and I saw at once that it was Peg Leg Pete.

Behind me I heard Mary gasp, "It's him!"

They had added the strength of their light beams to mine, as though by some magnetic magic the drake would be drawn to us.

But Pete slithered away, head extended, one leg pumping frantically, until he was lost among the cattails. I turned my light to the side of the muskrat house where he'd been sitting, and saw a darker stain which I knew at once was blood, and I knew now Pete would indeed have to be strong if he wasn't going to end up as something for the crows to quarrel about.

Back up at the house we went in through the bottom basement door. The children took off their boots, and I dropped my muddy, sopping clothing in a heap next to the shower stall.

Only when I was standing under the streams of hot water did the shivering subside. I had no dry clothes in the basement, so I went up with a towel around my middle, and got into my pajamas and a robe.

Everyone was at the kitchen table, and though they were sipping hot chocolate, nobody touched the popcorn which stood in the center of the table in a huge yellow bowl. Gwen had poured me a mug of hot coffee, and I lowered my face to it so I could feel the heat as the steam curled up over my chin and around my cheeks.

Nobody said a word, so I finally looked up, and said, "Well, it's something you've got to expect." The children just looked at me, and I had the feeling they thought I should accept the guilt for that generation of hunters which had crowded the river and shot at Pete.

But, of course, there had been men of all ages out on the river, and even some women, so how, I thought, could they think this hunting thing was one of those generation consequences. I felt anger rushing blood to my head, and I said, "Look, it's not the first time. You've lost dozens and dozens of.pets before, and if you insist on trying to help every injured animal or bird that comes along, you can expect you are going to have more moments like this." They lowered their eyes then, but still they didn't talk.

"Darn it!" I said, slamming my mug down so hard hot coffee splattered across the table, "You darn kids can't face up to anything. One small misadventure, a minor tragedy, and you sit around looking like the world's going to end. What are you going to do if life really slams you one below the belt?"

Of course, life had slammed both of them below the belt. Dianne had been six when her real father died, and Mary had been four when her real mother died. But this never occurred to me now, and maybe it was because I wasn't really so concerned with the way they felt, but because I, a grown man who had survived a terrifying war, the loss of a wife, and, of course, many fine friends, had let the life of one insignificant, no-account, one-legged bundle of almost worthless feathers move me to compassion.

It just didn't make sense. If I wanted to weep, the headlines in the paper every night could give me plenty to cry about, because the world was a cruel place of starving children, desolately lonely old people, war-torn men, women, and children . . . misfortune perpetually revolving on a cylindric kaleidoscope of obituaries. But maybe it was only that I felt so helpless. Or maybe I was angry because once again I was feeling death's clammy fingers testing the texture of my own skin.

Whatever, I acted savagely as a cornered rat which knows for sure the dog is going to kill it, and I didn't simmer down until I felt Gwen's hand press down on my arm.

Then I lowered my eyes, and I felt the heat drain away from in back of my eyes, and then when I could look up again I said:

"I'm sorry. We'll see what we can do tomorrow."

(14

That night I had a terrible dream. It was the beginning of an autumnal day, and in the dream the sun was a bloody splash on the horizon. Wherever I looked there were hunters. They stood elbow-to-elbow, waiting. Finally as the sun topped the horizon a whistle blew, and the army advanced, shooting.

Everything which scurried along the ground or managed to become airborne fell before their fire. Hawks, herons, swans, rabbits, pheasants, deer, opossums . . . none were spared.

They marched on and on through marsh after marsh, up into the woodlands and over the hills. They advanced through the valleys shoulder-to-shoulder, shooting.

Quail fell like flies caught in a gust of lethal spray. Robins, orioles, grackles, thrushes, chickadees . . . the earth was littered with their bodies.

Then I came awake. Sweat trickled down the middle of my back. I moved my arm to feel that my wife was still beside me, and that I was not, in fact, a part of the mob bent on raking the earth with shot. I went to the kitchen for a glass of warm milk, and when I opened the refrigerator, there were the bodies of the three ducks I had killed, pink now beneath protecting jackets of cellophane.

I sat at the kitchen table wide awake, and I knew sleep would be a long time in coming. So I thought about the dream, and I wondered what it meant—if anything.

Where had the real American sportsman gone, I wondered. Or was he still extant, and had the years only melted me down into a bleeding heart?

Then I thought about a lot of things while sitting there. I thought about the first any-deer season ever held in Wisconsin when a half million hunters crashed into the north woods, and I'd seen entire families fill their tag quotas with tiny fawns. I remembered coming across moose carcass after moose carcass in Canada— left to rot by hunters who had come only to collect a trophy head. I remembered an archery hunt held on icy Horicon Marsh during which hunters who couldn't pull a bow clubbed deer to death when they couldn't get back to their feet on the slick ice.

I remembered a goose hunt from public grounds where two hundred and twenty hunters, all wearing the arm bands which entitled them to hunt a refuge perimeter, fired, by conservation department count, twenty-two hundred shells to kill three geese and how nobody would even begin to guess how many had been hit to fly away and die.

I remembered a night on Lake Superior's Kakagon Sloughs when the shooting started after I was in bed, and after the moon had risen, and continued all night, and in the morning the place was crawling with cripples the violaters hadn't been able to pick up in the dark.

I thought about the president of a large conservation club, and how he had shot and hidden five bucks beneath brush piles and then came back on the last day of the season to select the largest, leaving the rest to rot.

Then I thought about Peg Leg Pete, and I thought about the three ducks in the refrigerator, and I thought about Mary and Dianne in their beds upstairs, and I thought about Debbie too, because she had arrived to spend Sunday at home.

It was stupid, of course, to sit there in the dim light counting all the sins of those who sometimes called themselves sportsmen. I'd drink a warm glass of milk and go back to bed.

Milk helped and I fell asleep, but the dream came right back, and the horde of hunters once more advanced abreast across the earth. And when they had passed there was only the sound of the cricket in the land. The trees were riddled, and the only sign of wildlife was an occasional animal track where the boots of the hunters had spared a small space of earth.

Then out of the void quite suddenly appeared all manner of trucks, graders, power shovels, bulldozers . . . all marked "Conservation Department," and they set out new brush piles, put up new hedges, replaced the riddled trees, and then after the habitat was in order, they released all manner of birds and animals.

By then I knew I was dreaming, so I tried to wake myself, and even though I fought it, I saw the hunters come again, and I saw the Conservation Department men selling them tickets, and then they lined up, and once more they began advancing across the refurbished terrain, shooting.

Then my wife awakened me. "Mel, you're screaming. What's the matter?"

I put my hand to my head. It was throbbing. "Bad dream," I said. "Just a bad dream. I'm all right."

She lay back down, and I closed my eyes, but I couldn't go back to sleep. So I got up and went down the carpeted hall and quietly up the carpeted steps.

I thought I hadn't made a sound, but I must have, because Dianne whispered, "Can't you sleep either?"

I said, "No. Guess I ate too much for supper."

"Maybe that's what it is," she said, "because I can't sleep either."

"Me either." It was Mary. She had heard us. Both girls slept in twin beds in the same room.

It was quiet then, because what was there to say. I walked quietly past their beds where a double window looks out on a thick stand of blue and Norway spruce, and juniper, maple and paper birch.

This is ridiculous, I thought, standing there. Here I was, a man who had seen scores die in bombing raids, a man who had helped drop enough bombs to wipe out a big city, a man who had gone out to kill people day after day and returned at night feeling no remorse . . . here I was, upset because a one-legged duck had gotten a bellyful of lead and was likely to die.

"This is crazy," I said, turning away from the window.

"What's going on in there?" It was Debbie from an adjoining room.

"Nothing," I said, "go back to sleep."

But she got up and came over, and she was a dim

126

figure with the tiny wall nightlight behind her in the hall. "Can't you guys let a person sleep?" she asked.

"I'm sorry," I said. "Who wants milk?"

I could hear both Dianne and Mary get up from their beds, but Debbie said, "I'm going back to sleep. I had a hard week."

Well, I'm sure she had had a hard week. School was getting rough, and she had entered and was now becoming a part of a new world, a world apart from Little Lakes and its muskrats and ducks and rabbits and robins.

In the kitchen I poured milk into a saucepan and put it on a burner. Dianne got a can of powdered chocolate from the cupboard, and we sat in the dim kitchen waiting for the milk to heat.

Then over hot cups of chocolate we talked about a lot of things. Dianne reminded me that we'd have to make an appointment for the horses to get their tetanus shots and to get wormed. And we agreed it was nearly time to get the snow plow on Bumpy and to get the snow tires on the car.

We wondered, too, if the winter would be hard, and whether or not Fish Pond would freeze out as it sometimes did. Dianne said it was time to put up the bird feeders and to get the squirrel feeder out of the back shed.

Mary wondered why it was that this year we had maybe twice the number of squirrels we'd had in any other year, and I explained it was because of the abundance of acorns.

"But what are they going to do when winter really comes?" she asked.

"We'll feed them. Then, too, some will scatter out to

other areas, and the weak or sick will of course die, as the weak and sick die every winter."

And it was the wrong thing to say, because I knew immediately they thought about Pete being down there bleeding, or perhaps already dead. But I didn't say anything, and finally Dianne noted that animals and birds sure had a rough time of it, and I agreed they often did have, but added:

"Except it doesn't bother them like it does you and me, because they don't contemplate the future. They live for this minute, and death is as natural for them as living. They just don't think about it, and so every minute of their lives is complete and there are no morbid thoughts keeping them awake at night."

We all laughed at that, and I suppose the tension broke. So I said, "Maybe we all ought to try to get some sleep. You two each want an aspirin to help you sleep?"

"Not me," Dianne said, "I'm not getting started on that stuff."

"Me either," Mary said. "I feel sleepy now."

I walked with them to the long hall which leads to the stairs, and then I turned and went into the bedroom.

"What on earth is going on out there?" Gwen asked.

"Oh, the kids got that crippled duck on their minds and they can't sleep. I just gave them some hot chocolate."

"Is that what's bothering you? That crippled duck?"

"Of course not."

"Well, something's bothering you."

"No, it's just one of those nights."

"Look't, Mel. This is Gwen. This is your wife you're talking to. So quit trying to be the hero."

I had to laugh at that. Then I said, "Well, maybe it

does bug me. But it isn't the crippled duck which bugs me so much, as the mystery of why I should be concerned about one individual bird when in a lifetime I've killed thousands."

"That's not hard to explain."

"Oh?"

"Well, just consider that there are hundreds of thousands of lonely old people in the world. Except you don't feel sorry for them individually because your life isn't intertwined with theirs. But you do feel sorry for Aunt Lee. Very personally sorry you can't make her happy."

And that was true. Aunt Lee was eighty-nine and blind and lived with another old woman, and at times they must have been very lonely and very sad, and we, in turn, felt very sad for them.

"It's more than that, though," I said.

"I suppose it is, but can't it wait until morning? What time is it anyway?"

"Two o'clock," I said.

"Good grief!"

"Okay. Okay."

"Come on. Cuddle up," she said.

It helped, but I was still a long, long time falling asleep, and I remember the two windows were becoming gray rectangles in the morning dawn before my mind finally said, "Now, Mel. Now. Please relax."

The children came to the ponds often, but they never saw Peg Leg. Then the ice came, and it was followed by snow. By the middle of January banks along the road were so high there was no place to push the snow, and we had to settle for a single lane, and when two cars met, one would have to back up to a turnoff to let the other vehicle pass.

The search for Pete became only a sometime thing, because by then we were certain his body was frozen fast in the ice somewhere beneath several feet of snow.

Except for that single night of sorrow, the children were not unduly upset. But that was the way it had to be. Death had long ago become a fact of life for them, and they could not afford the luxury of long periods of mourning.

Sometimes they talked about Pete, but with a detachment which reflected their maturity. Dianne hoped that the foxes had found the drake, because "in that way his death will have served some good purpose. He will have fed the foxes."

Mary, however, was a little too young to wish for that

kind of an end for the mallard. She hoped, if he had died, that the end had come peacefully along the edge of the creek where his body might add to the luster of the marsh marigolds when they goldplated the stream banks in spring.

Debbie, of course, thought her sisters were what she called, "out of their skulls." Her world had changed. She was taking part in war protests, was an ardent and voluble crusader for women's rights, and she had gone from dresses to blue jeans, and from ribbons to leather fringe. Her one strong attachment to Little Lakes remained her horse, Rebel Red. It was going to take a strong love to take precedent.

But even had we wanted to mourn, there never would have been time for it. There rarely is time, even for proper reflection, when a northern winter decides to test a people. And we were being tested.

Our January thaw brought rain, but not much, only enough to soak the snowbanks. Then it froze again, and the banks became hard as iron. The freeze was followed by a sixteen-inch snow.

Some trails were beyond opening. Even Bumpy, with its gears set to turn all four wheels, finally got stuck and we had to dig to get it out.

So the trail to the stable remained closed, and the children had to scramble over drifts a hundred yards to feed the horses. Then they had to go on for another couple of hundred yards to dig the ice out of the water hole, and the shores of Fish Pond became so slippery the horses often settled to their front knees while drinking, so they wouldn't slide into the hole.

The snow in the dog runs was so deep, the dogs walked right out over the fences, and again the children had to dig and throw out snow to keep them back of wire.

The one-lane plank bridge over Watercress Creek became hazardous to plow, so we shoveled it out first, and then eased Bumpy across.

Snow around the house itself became a problem, so we locked the front door, and let the drifts pile up there, and only kept paths open to the sun-room door and the basement.

What's more, we kept the fireplace in the living room and the one in the basement burning almost constantly. It wasn't, of course, because we needed the extra heat, because the furnace was adequate, but because the leaping flames were a bright reflection of our ability to meet winter at its worst.

In fact, the basement fireplace burned for a month without going out, and then we decided to see how long we could keep a fire in it. We put logs on just before going to bed, and then again on awakening in the morning, and I began announcing in my Sunday column how many hours and days and weeks the fire had been burning. When it finally went out because a green log leaked sap into the flames, it had been burning for more than twenty weeks, almost two thousand and four hundred hours.

In addition to its being fun, there was such reassurance from our open fires as can only be explained by our primitive beginnings. Maybe the flames gave us assurance because, perhaps, there lurks in all of us an aboriginal need not only to feel the warmth, but to see the flames suck up the chimney, to hear the comfortable crackle of wood as it burns.

Anyway, we ate deeply into the woodpiles in the

basement, and by February we were hauling chunks from the reserves in the stable and the shed behind the garage.

Then one day, when I saw it still wasn't going to be enough, I said to Gwen, "I'm going to knock down a couple of dead trees."

"I suppose you should," she agreed, but then added, "but with all this snow it'll be tough."

So we beat paths to an elm which I had always been afraid to drop because of wires and other trees which were crowding it. I put the chain saw to the wood and it snarled and began chewing greedily into the trunk, and I had planned right, because the tree settled into the notch I made and fell without bringing down any wires and without damaging any of the young cedars below.

A small cheer went up from Gwen and the two girls, and then we tackled the downed tree, sawing even the little limbs into fireplace lengths.

It was really no great thing. We'd cut down, brushed out and chunked up a couple of hundred trees on the place. But that night after supper when we were all in the living room around the fireplace, we all seemed to be the stronger for it.

"People are strange creatures," I said, from my big leather chair which stands in a corner where I can reach my favorite books standing on shelves on either side.

"Why do you say that?" Gwen asked.

"Well, people all talk about peace, contentment, leisure . . . the lazy life. But the fact is they're always at their best when they've got an opponent, when there's a challenge to be met."

133

She thought a moment, and said, "Of course. That's why a country can be so united when at war."

"Well, why can't they be united in peace against such things as poverty, pollution, cancer . . . all kinds of things?" Dianne asked.

"Maybe that day is coming, too," I said.

"Well, I wish it would hurry up," Dianne said.

"It might. The signs are out."

"You think so?" Gwen asked. She was serious, concerned.

I wanted to think so. I wanted to think so because I wanted to hold forth some promise for my children. I wanted the children to think that before they died they might see a more perfect world than my parents could have ever dreamed was possible.

In answer to Gwen's question, I only said, "Well it will take foresight and work."

"What about courage?" Dianne asked. "What about just plain guts?"

"That's built in. Courage is there. It is the child of survival. When we need it we get it. Just take Pete for instance. He didn't have to have courage or to think about surviving. The courage came to him as naturally as breathing. It was necessary to his life. So we call him courageous."

"I still think some people don't have it," Dianne said.

But by then the rest of us were thinking of Pete, and nobody challenged her statement. And I thought that perhaps if Pete had only been a little less courageous, he might have stayed on the ponds where it was safe.

I didn't put forth the proposition that a courageous act can also sometimes be a foolhardy act. I'm sure the children knew that, because, having been thrown from their horses more than a few times, they learned not to put the animals over jumps they weren't likely to be able to maneuver.

Outside, the temperature was below zero, and the picture window which had been put in long years before thermo panes became the thing, had frosted out from all its edges to put a lacy white frame around the snow-covered spruce which the spotlight on the house held in bright focus.

The children moved away from the fire then, but they never stayed away too long, and if they had work in some other part of the house, they drifted back from time to time, if only to look at the flames.

Winter was a long time in wearing down, but finally the assaults of spring became a little too much for it, and the snow began to melt. It started slowly, with a little slush around noon of every day. It returned relentlessly then, until some days the eaves were dripping and there was water running in the ditches and the ice on the ponds became honeycombed waiting only for a strong wind to break it into so many bright shards.

So through March and into April, winter retreated and then attacked, retreated and came back, but each time it tried to recapture the land it did so with less and less enthusiasm.

By now, of course, everyone in the village and some other people throughout Wisconsin and the Middle West knew that Peg Leg Pete was missing. They saw it in my Sunday column in the *Milwaukee Journal*, though I hadn't written about how I had almost shot him, nor had I written about how he had come home wounded.

135

I only wrote that he was missing and left it at that. Maybe that is because every time I write about such things as the depredations of cats, or how we trap muskrats, or how I go out to shoot ducks or pheasants . . . I get a lot of letters from people who accuse me of being everything from a heartless scoundrel to a sadist.

So you learn, especially if you've been a writer for a great many years, that sometimes things are best not mentioned, most especially in newspaper columns or magazine articles.

But it's quite different with books. I'm not sure if I know all the reasons why. But it is different, and when you write a book you put in all kinds of things which you would never even consider putting in a column.

In that way books are often much more honest than newspapers and magazines. If a character in a book uses a four-letter word, why you have him use it, because he *did* say it, and you can't help but put down what he said. But in a newspaper or a magazine, of course, the editor would take out the naughty word, and have your character say something which, of course, he never would say.

I suppose it is because newspapers and even magazines are sometimes almost forced upon us. I suppose it is because they are family things, like talk around the kitchen table where you watch your language. What's more, we have to read newspapers and magazines if we want to know what's going on in the world—even if too often, the magazines or newspapers don't know themselves.

But with a book it's different. There's more deliberation. Books do not arrive every day or every week, but you decide among some thirty thousand which are published each year and then you can go out and buy them.

Anyway, as I started to write, a lot of people were well acquainted with Peg Leg, even if they didn't know all the facts, and I got letters from a lot of places and a couple of letters were even addressed to Peg Leg Pete himself.

So it was, of course, incumbent upon me to put Pete to rest, once and for all. I didn't quite know how to do it, because, as they say in police circles, there was no corpus delicti.

Anyway, one Sunday early in May, when all the spring flowers were making Little Lakes lovely, I sat in my big, brown chair and took my pencil, and made ready to end the saga of Peg Leg Pete.

I did a lot of pencil chewing, and Gwen brought me coffee three times, and all I had written on the paper which was attached to a clipboard which I balanced on my knee, was: "Page 1."

Noon came and went, and the house became empty and quiet because Gwen had joined all three children outside (Debbie was home) to count the flowers, and to stand watching the black bass on their white pebble nests, and marvel at the multicolored mating costumes of the bluegills, and hear the cardinals whistling and the blackbirds cheering.

Then I finally wrote, "It is safe to assume, by now, that Peg Leg Pete, the mallard drake who lost his leg to a muskrat trap, was the victim of one of the most severe winters to have ever visited southern Wisconsin. Now that the ponds are all open . . ."

The telephone rang, and I stopped writing. It rang again, but I didn't get up because I was accustomed to having someone else answer it. When it rang the fifth time I got up and went to the next room to answer it.

It was Jerry Washicheck, Sr., the octogenarian who is my neighbor, and who has a pond right in his front yard. (Jerry died at eighty-five while I was writing this book.)

"Mel, you got a minute?"

"Of course," I said.

"Well, come on over. I've got something to show you."

In a way I was glad to be rid of the clipboard and the white paper which seems always to be hungry for words. On the sun porch I looked across the long sweep of lawn. Mary and Dianne were swimming in Blue Pool, though I knew the water had to be freezing.

I went out and down the road past the house of Jerry's son, Red, and then across to Grandpa Washicheck's place. There, standing together on the slope of lawn, was Jerry, Sr., and his wife and Red and his wife, and they were throwing corn and bread to a gathering of five mallard drakes.

I wondered if that was what Jerry had called me to see, because, of course, I'd often seen him feed the ducks, and it was no thing with which to disturb a man's Sunday.

"Look. Look," Red said.

I did, and then I saw one of the drakes which had been flat on its belly, lurch forward to get a piece of bread.

It was Peg Leg Pete!

(16

It was the spring of nineteen hundred and seventy, and after alerting the rest of the family to the fact that Pete was back, I went into the house and wrote:

"Peg Leg Pete is back, ressurrected as it were, from the dead. This morning he came with four other drakes to accept bread and corn after having been away since last fall.

"Where he spent the winter has got to be pure conjecture. When we last saw him he was a sick duck, slithering through the cattails, blood leaking from shotgun wounds inflicted during a foolhardy flight to the Fox River on the opening day of the 1969 duck hunting season.

"He could fly, of course, else how in the first place would he have made it back to Little Lakes after having been shot? So perhaps when the ice began creeping up from the Mill Pond into the marsh in which he had sought sanctuary, he joined some southbound flock.

"We don't know, of course, if that is the case. The last time we saw him he didn't look strong enough to lift his head, much less fly.

"Except we know he didn't winter at Little Lakes. There was no open water except along a small section of Watercress Creek, and he couldn't have survived in any other corner of these acres because the snow was piled high even over the ice.

"It is possible, of course, that he made it south. When the ice arrived here, he might have found an open river fifty miles south. Then when the ice came creeping down to that river, perhaps he flew farther to where another river offered open water.

"Hedge hopping in this manner, always out front of the cold and snow, he might ultimately have reached southern Illinois, or gone on into Missouri or even Arkansas.

"If this is what happened, his must have been an heroic retreat. With only one leg, with shotgun pellets perhaps burning in his breast, with hunger pinching his craw, with sleet and snow combining to drive him back down to the frozen places, only a courageous heart would have pumped enough strength to keep weary wings from faltering.

"At the expense of being called an anthropomorphic bleeding heart, I've got to believe that it took some sort of extraordinary kind of courage, some special effort beyond the basic laws governing survival.

"Now if this is true, then it is contrary to what I have always told my children. I have said, when we talked, that courage in the animal world is no great thing, but only a child of survival. That when the the need to fight for life presents itself to an animal or bird, courage is a spontaneous thing.

"I think I must amend that now to say that among animals there seems to be many kinds of courage, just

140

as there are many kinds of survival, some of which do not even have anything to do with physical death.

"I've got to admit . . ."

And then I stopped writing. I was getting into deep water, into the realm of the metaphysical, a field I was about as qualified to explore as Peg Leg himself.

So I took the two pages of copy I had written, shoved them into the bottom drawer of my desk, and got on with writing very simply that Peg Leg Pete had somehow survived the severe winter and was back and apparently healthy and happy.

Of course, that night at supper no one talked about anything except Pete. Even Debbie, who after nearly a year in Milwaukee was back to wearing dresses occasionally, and back to visiting the ponds around the place, had no caustic comment, but was genuinely happy the duck had survived, that he was back.

But, of course, now that Debbie's brief age of cynicism had run its teenage course, it was Dianne's turn to be the young skeptic. So when I said something about Pete being a great one, she said something like, "Oh, I don't know. Ducks are ducks are ducks."

I looked at Gwen and she gave me a curt nod. The nod meant that now we'd have to go through another period of adolescent sophistry, and then just about the time Dianne got her feet back on the ground, Mary would, in her turn, become, if not the family's young Sophocles, then surely our sophomoric sage. Gwen said it was a predictable and as critical a part of growing as the purchase of a girl's first bra and a boy's first razor.

But if all this seems a little aside from the story of Peg Leg Pete, be assured that it isn't. Pete was as much an influence on especially the philosophical development of all of us as any professor could possibly be.

As for Pete, he had changed. No longer did he sit far off and wait while the other ducks gobbled the corn which had been spread, but now he swam among them fighting as hard as any for his share.

What's more, if he wasn't accepted by the society of ducks, he was tolerated, because he could hit as hard with his bill as any, and that ended the segregation.

By the time Pete had showed up again at Little Lakes, all the hens had been spoken for, and most were already laying olive eggs in nests of dry grass and down, and I expect some were already incubating.

So there was nothing for Pete except the bachelor colony of four semi-wild mallard drakes, and, of course, Salt and Pepper, both of whom had no desire to mate to begin with.

In due time then, the bouncy, bronze duckling clutches began to appear on the ponds, and then the bachelor colony got new members as the hens, done with their husbands, sent them packing.

For Pete, life seemed to smooth out. He looked splendid, especially if there was a sun to strike emerald reflections from his shiny green head into the water. All the ducks, in fact, floated about in flocks of quiet contentment.

School let out. Shoes came off. Windows of the house stood wide. Dinners were sometimes enjoyed on the front lawn. The pale flowers of spring faded, only to be replaced by the more brazen blooms of summer.

Debbie worked days for a neighbor, and Dianne and Mary had charge of keeping the grass mowed at Little Lakes, of hauling pond water to the new trees, of pruning adolescent trees, and then sometimes helping me when I'd drop a couple of dead or dying trees for fireplace wood. But every afternoon after work we all ended up in Blue Pool to cool off after our day of labor.

Summer behaved. There was just enough rain, but not too much, and there was plenty of sunshine and the spruce put up long spires of new growth and the pines put up tall candles. The frogs were loud at night, and we fell asleep hypnotized by the rhythm of their syncopated singing.

With such idyllic days and nights all given to growth, it was difficult to remember that death never takes a holiday. It was only if you looked close that you might notice a blood spot on a blade of grass where an owl had lifted a mouse, or a crayfish armor, hidden in the deep grass where a coon had dined. But, of course, the spiders all had their nets stretched, and the little green herons were spearing fish and frogs, and the dragonflies on flashing wings were hunting every watery alley for insects.

But in summer you don't think about death the way you do in winter, and especially not this summer because there were no hawks. Then even if we heard the kingfisher's rattling war cry as he streaked like a blue arrow to kill a small bass, we admired the bird and forgot about the fish.

Maybe that's why we like summer all out of proportion to winter. In winter if there is a kill, there are the blood stains and the evidence of a struggle in the snow. In summer flowers cover the evidence, like wreaths are meant to hide a casket so a funeral becomes more bearable.

So, of course, if summer is the season of rebirth, the

price of being born is the same, and there is no special time to make the payment. So sometimes we were given sharp reminders, as when we heard a frog's last terrifying croak as the snake struck, or heard a young rabbit scream in the night as the fox closed its jaws over it.

Then one night it was the ducks. It was sometime after midnight, and the persistent quacking of a hen down on one of the ponds awakened me. But the ducks quacked often in the night, so I tried to go back to sleep. But the quacking of the single hen persisted, and then as if something had triggered all the ducks, there was a wild cacophony of sound, and I'm sure it was so loud it was heard up in the village, and perhaps even in the subdivision to the east of us.

I raised up in bed and when Gwen asked, "What's the matter?" I said, "Something is after the ducks."

"Well, don't you think you ought to go down?"

I was going to say that something is probably always stalking the ducks, and to inquire why it was she thought I should go down at that time of the night, when there were shadows in the doorway of our bedroom.

So I slipped trousers over my pajama bottoms, and followed by Dianne and Mary still in their summertime shorty pajamas, started off across the grass with three flashlights swinging wild arcs of light up and down and across the lawn.

The racket was coming from the Mill Pond, and we hurried through a small stand of spruce, now shoulder-high, and we all focused our lights in the direction of the quacking.

There was a large gathering of ducks around a tiny

island which was completely overgrown with night-shade. All the ducks except one were in the water. That one, a mallard hen, was on the island and a mink had her by a wing elbow and was holding fast.

It was obvious that before our arrival the mink had gotten in some telling bites on other parts of the duck's body, because she was fighting but feebly. The ducks in the water were all quacking at the top of their voices, and now and again one or another would charge only to break off the rescue attempt just short of the target.

On shore we began shouting to distract the mink. But the animal, a long, large, almost-black lance of fur had no intention of letting its supper get away.

"If only we had a boat," Mary said.

"Let's drag one over from Fish Pond," Dianne said.

"No, wait!" I said sharply.

Peg Leg Pete had come swimming out of the rushes toward the island. I wanted to see what he would do. I don't know, but I can't believe I was hoping to get evidence that there really were special kinds of courage, even among animals.

Well, I didn't have long to wait. Pete came swimming swiftly as his one leg would permit. Then a dozen feet from the mink, he vaulted into the air, and incredibly, he hurled himself like a javelin at the mink.

The wonder of it is that he didn't snap the mink's back. He hit the animal with his bone-hard bill, and I was sure I could hear ribs cracking. It was enough for the mink. With a scream of rage he let go, and the hen went scuttling across the surface of the pond.

The mink swam then, and the whole duck flock followed, still protesting, but at a safe distance. Only Pete remained behind, squatting on the island of night-shade, and he didn't slide back off into the water until after the mink disappeared among the cattails and the ducks were quiet once again.

(17

Next day I went down early with the children to survey the duck flock, and we could distinguish the hen which had been attacked because some of her wing feathers were still in disarray. She was herding a clutch of ducklings back out of a marsh pocket where snapping turtles were likely to lurk.

Pete was there, too, and maybe it was only our imagination, or perhaps wishful thinking, but he seemed to hold himself higher in the water, swim with what looked like such confidence as heroic acts can sometimes engender.

"He looks cocky," Dianne said.

"For a fact, he does," I agreed.

On the way back to the house we detoured a little to have a look in a sheltered place surrounded by spruce and red pine. We called it Gwen's Corner, because it was a special place reserved by her for transplanting wild flowers rescued from the concrete thrust of freeways.

Most of the flowers were spring flowers, and already their blooms had faded. But on some long, straight stems there still hung lavender and white shooting stars, and violets put out fringes of white around spruce skirts, and on lower ground some purple violets still bloomed, and, of course, all the varieties of daisies were now opening.

A cottontail appeared suddenly, ran a few rods, and sat and with ears stiffly at attention, watched, hoping we wouldn't find the tiny, round nest in the ground where there were young she'd obviously been nursing.

"Should we look for the nest?" Dianne asked.

"Let's," Mary said.

Very carefully, so we wouldn't step where the young lay hidden in a hollow, fur-lined cup in the earth, we searched. But *knowing* a rabbit may have a nest but a few feet away, and *finding* it, are two different things. We were about to give up when Mary said, "Guess what!"

"Okay," Dianne said, "I give up. What?"

"Come look."

So we did, and there, beneath spruce boughs sat a brown mallard hen obviously still incubating eggs.

"She's sure late," Dianne said.

"Probably lost her first clutch," I explained.

Then while we looked the bright-eyed, buff head of a very tiny duckling popped out from under a wing.

"The eggs are hatching. Right now!" I said.

As many times as the children had seen births occur, it continued to be a miraculous thing for them, and to hear their expressions of surprise, you might think they were witnessing it for the first time.

We backed off then, because the hen had crouched lower and was moving restlessly, and we didn't want her to put a flat, webbed foot down on a still wet youngster and suffocate it before it had a chance to peep forth and let the brightness in its eyes be lighted by the sun.

"Maybe we'd better let her be," I said.

"She does seem awful restless. Probably really a wild one," Dianne said.

("Wild ones" were new arrivals. Having been in residence a few months and consenting to accept corn, ducks were generally considered "tame.")

So we backed off, and I left the children to get on up to the house where such a multitude of tasks awaited me, I was often at a loss to know which piece of writing ought to be given priority.

I had three books, one juvenile and two adult, in various stages of completion. I had only recently contracted with Associated Press to do a nationally syndicated column called the "Good Earth Crusade." Then, of course, there was my Sunday *Milwaukee Journal* column, articles for several magazines which still requested them, the mail, and sometimes I gave talks, so I had to keep a variety of speeches up-to-date for a wide range of audiences—adult and juvenile.

So I tried to clear my mind of all extraneous things, such as ducks and flowers and inquiring children, and get on with a book I was doing.

Except the words wouldn't come, and there as always was the white page of paper, waiting it seemed almost anxiously, but once again, there was nothing written on it except: "Page 1."

Other writers who were friends and acquaintances of mine rented offices and traveled to them daily, because they claimed they couldn't get anything written while trying to work where family life throbbed about them. I had tried working in a small cabin which stands on the shore of Clear Pool, but the children gravitated to it as though I were a magnet and they were iron filings. Then I had coverted a coal bin in the basement into an office and soundproofed it, but the quarters were so small I began exhibiting signs of claustrophobia, and so I converted it into a file room, and moved back up to my easy chair in the living room.

And that's where I was when at noon the children came to tell me it was time for lunch, and I still hadn't given the word-hungry white page anything with which to satisfy its voracious appetite.

"She had nine ducklings," Mary announced, as we came to the kitchen table.

"Are they out of the nest?" I asked.

"Yup," Mary said.

"She's got them down on Clear Pool," Dianne added.

"All the eggs hatch?" I asked.

"All but one," Mary said. "We're going to open it."

"Not around the house," I said. "If it's rotten we'll smell it for a month."

I saw Mary give Dianne one of her secret looks, so I asked, "Where's the egg?"

Mary looked down at her plate. I stared directly at Dianne. "In the sun-room," she said.

I turned, and from my chair I could see out into the sun-room, and there the egg sat on the glass topped table.

"If that egg breaks in here and stinks up my house, I'll whip you both," Gwen said.

"Why did you have to bring it in?" I asked.

"We were afraid if we left it outside something might get at it."

"Look," I said, "don't you kids ever learn?"

150

They should have learned by this time, of course, because they'd blown the contents from more than one abandoned egg by pricking both ends. They should have learned because they'd run into enough rotten ones to last a demonstrator through any rally. They should have learned because one of their rotten eggs had exploded in the heat of the sun on a ledge in the sun-room, and now two years later, you could still smell rotten eggs when you went into that corner.

"We'll take it out right after lunch," Dianne promised.

"You'd better. And don't drop it if you know what's good for you," Gwen added.

After we'd eaten, I went back to my brown leather chair, and my blank piece of paper. I could hear Gwen rattling dishes in the kitchen sink, and I could hear the children giggling as they went past a window. But I tried not listening, tried to put the children, the ducks, Little Lakes . . . everything out of my mind, and finally I started writing:

"The lingering perfume of her presence was still on the steps, and at first Silk came every day to look for her. In the beginning, she hadn't waited for the cover of night, but came trotting down the sidewalk each morning to take her place upon the porch."

My pencil stopped. The story I was writing was about how a dog named Silk had managed to survive in a big city for a year without ever being caught. I had entitled it, *Gutter Runner*, but I was having trouble, sitting out here in the country, visualizing how it would be for the dog downtown among the crush of buildings, the crush of people and automobiles.

So I tried mesmerizing myself, making believe I was

right down there in the middle of the city, and it was working. I could hear the din of traffic, smell the exhaust fumes, see the hurrying faces, and then from the sun-room to break the spell came Dianne's voice, "Dog! Dog!"

I tried to ignore her, to keep my mind downtown where my character, Silk, would have to contend with such dangers as no country dog might ever dream of.

But Dianne persisted, "Dog! Dog!", and then when I didn't answer to my nickname, she called, "Dad! Dad!"

So the spell was broken. The city I had contrived to create in my mind dissolved. I was back in the country. With a gesture of defeat, I tossed the clipboard to the brown footstool, put the pencil back on the tray where my other sharpened pencils lay, and went out to the sun-room.

"What is it?" I asked, somewhat brusquely.

"The egg. It's got a duck in it. It's alive!"

I looked at Mary who was standing silent beside her older sister. She nodded vigorously, and her big, brown eyes were shining like plump ripe olives as they come dripping from the jar.

So I went out, across the back lawn, down the path beneath the hickory, and through some oaks to the back of the pet compound.

There, in a shroud of egg white, amidst a fragment of shells, a duckling lay looking like a brown, wet rag. I knelt, and as I did my mind made a startling leap back over the many decades of my life to another duckling which had lain amidst the wreckage of its olive shell.

I saw that other duckling, wet and somewhat bloodied, but still struggling for life. I saw the tiny eyes of this other fragment of life, even its tiny webbed feet.

152

I saw my father kneeling. I saw him reach out for a piece of cordwood, saw the club lift and then descend to crush the life from the duckling.

As if by instinct I looked around for a club, and Mary and Dianne caught the significance of my glance, and I heard them gasp. So I looked back at the duckling, poked it with a finger, saw it move.

"Get me some rags. Some cotton."

They were away like wind-driven leaves, and back even before I'd had a chance to relight the pipe which had gone cold in my hands.

Carefully then, I sopped up some of the egg white, lifted the duckling to wrap it in cotton, and then carried it to the sun-room.

Where the sun came warmly through a southern window I put the cotton-swaddled duckling so the heat could further dry its down. Then we sat to watch.

Mostly, I suppose, it was like watching a flower unfold in a timed film exposure. Bit by bit, parts of the duckling responded. First the tiny feet. Then the head. Then the wing stubs. One side dried, and fluffed out, so I turned the duckling to dry the other side.

"Looks like it didn't have an egg tooth," I said, "and that's maybe why it couldn't crack the shell." And it was true, the duckling did not have the usually tiny "tooth" on the end of its bill for cracking its way out of an egg shell.

Within a half hour the duckling was on its somewhat unsteady feet, and then it peeped. The peep was the signal the children must have been waiting for. I could hear them expel air from their lungs as though they'd been holding their breaths during the entire awakening. I half-expected them to cheer, but they didn't.

153

They only whispered as though the sound of their voices might be too much of a shock for an unfolding life.

"He's beautiful." It was Gwen. She had been standing behind the children watching.

"Yeah, pretty enough," I said, getting up. "Give him another hour," I said, "and then take him down and see if his mother will accept him."

I went back to my writing, but it was no good. Though I'd lived in the city for enough years to envisage just how it was, I couldn't stimulate the magic it takes to get back there now and get on with writing my story about Silk.

So I put the clipboard away, put the pencil down, lighted my pipe and went through the sun-room and on down the sweep of lawn to the ponds.

I could hear the children over on Clear Pool so I went through the spruce and broke out into the clearing. When they saw me, Dianne said, "The mother won't take him. She chases him."

I came to the bank to watch. The duckling was floating high like a well-dried curl of brown leaf. Its brothers and sisters were in a tight huddle of tiny bodies next to the mother.

Then each time the duckling we had saved from death approached the clutch composed of its brothers and sisters, the hen drove it away.

"What are we going to do?" Mary asked.

"Catch him and take him back up to the house," I said.

"But how?" Dianne asked.

"Drag a skiff over."

"All the way from Fish Pond?" Dianne asked.

And so I helped, and we skidded the skiff up to a road which runs around the hill, and there we loaded it on Bumpy and took it down to Clear Pool.

Straining and sweating we dragged it through the brush willow, and then with Dianne paddling furiously, and Mary wielding a huge landing net fashioned for lifting fish, they snared the rejected duckling, and between tender palms carried it back to the house.

(18

Nights the duckling was kept in a box in the basement. Daytimes it spent outside imprisoned by a small circle of chicken wire. The girls scooped a hole in the earth, put a small pan into it, and filled it with water for a swimming pool.

The duckling thrived. It ate water-warmed mash, chased flies and mosquitos, and then by the time its pinfeathers began to sprout began taking whole corn. It was a hen, a small, svelte hen, and she reminded me of the duck, Lily, who so many many years ago had thought she was people and had ridden without anchor on the waters of Rock River out among my other live decoys.

So I suggested to the girls they call her Lily. "Lily? Lily!" Dianne said. "What kind of name is that for a duck?"

"Well," I said, "you've had ducks named Aristotle, Plato, not to mention Silver. So what's so strange about calling her Lily?"

"It just sounds so, well you know, old-fashioned."

Of course, it really didn't make any difference to me,

but as a writer I had what amounted to a passion for seeing things come full circle, being neatly tied off. But, of course, life isn't like that. There are always loose ends, ragged edges, and so only in the novel, if the author wills it, can life be tied neatly into a bow.

But the children *did* call the duck Lily, and then when she had her feathers, they moved her into the pet compound where, at the time, there was a collection of some fifteen or more painted turtles—all with names— a pair of ringnecked pheasants, the woodchuck, such an assortment of rabbits I can only remember that one was called Grandma, and, of course, an assortment of ducks.

The pets were segregated according to species, so Lily went in with the ducks. But it was an unhappy arrangement. Waddle, an over-sexed and egocentric male, pursued Lily constantly. Then when he tired of trying to pin the little brown hen down, a jealous Greta took to making Lily's life miserable.

So, in the end, Lily went back to her own piece of private wire where she was safe from the hissing, kissing drake and the clucking white hen.

By then summer was beginning to fade. The bright new springtime shine had gone from the leaves, and they hung lifeless and sometimes a few even flew in the hot southerly wind. The lindens began dropping their bracts and their hard, little nutlike fruits, and the hickories began to rag. Green pond weeds turned bronze, and the fish left the warm shallows and congregated in the spring holes. The ducks on the ponds were mostly quiet, still not fully recovered from the molt, and spring songs of most of the birds were rarely heard.

Alone in her prison, Lily seemed disconsolate. She sat hunched up, rarely flapped her wings, and the bright

157

sparkle left her eyes. The children sometimes took turns sitting with her hoping that would help, and then when it didn't, they turned her loose on the hill and she took to following them around wherever they went.

I was, of course, reminded of the original Lily all over again. It was amazing, of course, but still understandable. This Lily, never having had a mother figure to follow, must have felt an affinity for the children, appointed them her surrogate mother.

Perhaps that had been the reason why the original Lily had thought she was people. I couldn't know, because among all the mallards and English callers which we raised, only those finally selected to become decoys took on individual identity in our eyes. But, of course, by the time they did, they were already grown and separated from the rest of the flock whose destiny was the oven.

School for the children came, just as taxes and death do to parents, and then one day in September they walked the long road to the top of the hill to catch the bus and Lily was alone.

My book, *Gutter Runner*, was well off the ground, and I had brought some system to writing my column by producing them in bursts of four at a time. The mail had slacked off as it does every summer, and the telephone rang less often, so I had more of every afternoon to spend fishing one or another of the ponds, and walking with Gwen around Little Lakes to discuss next spring's planting.

Naturally, I spent some time with Lily, but if I found nostalgic memories of another duck of long, long ago heightening my desire to form a closer and more satisfactory relationship with the little brown hen, Lily proved to be a reluctant lover.

She would take corn from me, and more especially angleworms and trout entrails, but she refused to follow me about, refused to welcome me with excited quacking, and began to sulk in a fence corner where a flaming sumac bent a leafy roof.

When the children came home from school, she would come alive, and if I was in my brown chair writing, I would know by her loud quacking that one or another of the youngsters was coming up the drive.

The days shortened, of course, and it wasn't long and once again Dianne and Mary got up before the sun to leave for school, just as each evening they did chores with flashlights.

So Lily's contact with them lessened, and she took to pouting most of every day, and if I'd get up from my chair to look out, I might see her sitting in a pitiful huddle beneath the sumac arbor, or listlessly plodding about the lawn.

What's more, since being given her freedom, the three dogs had been kept confined, and being deprived of their daily half-hour of exercise made them fractious and noisy.

The children were aware, of course, that Lily was unhappy. Often at night they'd carry her into the basement, and sit with her awhile, before turning her back out onto the lawn.

"Think we ought to lock her in a private pen next to Waddle and Greta?" Dianne asked.

"Well, it'd give the dogs a chance to run. Are there any pens open?"

"There's one she could have, but we'd have to move a couple of rabbits."

Moving rabbits isn't as easy as it sounds. If you put two bucks together the fur flies and then there is always one or another being brought to the kitchen for first aid. But if you put the bucks with the does . . . Well, we needed more rabbits like we needed more leaves on the lawn.

"Maybe she should go down to the ponds with the others," I suggested.

"I don't know," Mary said. "Something might get her. She's not used to being on her own, and it gets kind of wild down there once in a while."

"What you say is true," I agreed, "but what else? She sure isn't happy up here."

No one said anything after that, and I dropped the subject. I knew now they would think about it, and then in a day or two or in a week, they would come to me with their decision.

Meanwhile frost came one night to whiten the lawn, and all the next day leaves twirled on the wind. The ducks in the pond were in a frenzy at the prospects of migration, even though most would not give in to the almost overwhelming urge to join a southbound flock.

The weekend came and the children hadn't made up their minds. All day Saturday they raked leaves and piled them into various corners of the pet compound to provide shelter against the winter which was bearing down on Wisconsin.

Still no word from Mary or Dianne about the duck, and Debbie, home for the weekend, kept her thoughts to herself, because little by little she was leaving us, and little by little she was becoming a part of another world into which she would soon step as a full-fledged adult.

There was a teachers convention that week. Teachers from all over the state converged on Milwaukee, and so there was no school Thursday or Friday.

Early in the week the temperature plummeted to fifteen degrees, and the ground froze hard as iron, and there was a skim of ice jutting out from the shores of several of the ponds.

I had just finished the first draft of *Gutter Runner,* so when Thursday came and the children were home, I took the day off and walked with them around Little Lakes to see where the muskrats were working on the dikes.

The colony of ducks had moved off Mill Pond to where Watercress Creek never froze and the water was always warm because the springs bubbled from the ground. Pete was with the flock, and he was not the same obsequious Pete we had once known, but as Dianne put it, "He's a really cool guy. He's one *gung ho* duck!"

We watched, and when another drake swam near, he braced and thrust his bill forward, and when a hen swam alongside he played at courting. Sometimes he lifted a little way into the air and then came slanting down to go skimming like a water skier.

While we were standing watching the ducks sporting on the blue water in the silvery sunshine, Mary said, "I think Lily could be happy down here."

"Maybe," Dianne said, "but look how long it took Pete. But anyway, what's the difference. She's just another duck." It was like her to be concerned and then like her to depreciate the very concern she felt. Her feelings seemed to be ambivalent. One day sympathetic, understanding. Then the next day worldly, cynical. It was her time of passage.

"There's one big difference between Pete and Lily," I said.

"What's that?" Mary asked.

"Well, when Pete was put out to shift for himself he was a cripple."

"That may be true," Dianne contended, "but it's also true that Lily was raised by hand. She's not accustomed to a duck society. She's a people duck."

(A people duck or a people woodchuck or a people raccoon or even a people wolf or anything prefixed by people, was one of the normally wild ones which had lived so long in captivity that it had become human oriented and was at a loss to adjust to the companionship of its own kind.)

"But what else?" I asked, somewhat sharply. "She just sits up there and mopes when you kids aren't home. Think of a whole winter during which she'll rarely see you except behind the rays of a flashlight because you'll not be home during daylight hours."

Neither Mary nor Dianne said anything after that. We continued our inspection of the dikes, and where a muskrat had burrowed we drove in a tall willow stake to mark the spot.

When we came to Clear Pool there was clean gravel below the dam on the creek bottom so we knew that 'rats had been trying to tunnel beneath the concrete apron.

"If they get through, the pond will wash right down the creek," I said.

It was, of course, a dangerous place to set traps, since the ducks congregated there in the fast water because it never froze. But we could make the traps duck-proof, by looping willow wands over them. The muskrats would swim through to get caught, but the ducks would turn away from the obstruction.

It took most of the morning to mark the places where the muskrats were doing damage, but we set no traps because the season was still ten days away.

That afternoon I answered mail, and the children drifted away to the homes of friends. Then that night when they were feeding the dogs, Buck got out and having had an eye on Lily from behind wire, he headed straight for her.

No amount of shouting prevailed, and the big black retriever was on the little duck in a long leap.

Lily must have been terrified. Buck weighed eighty pounds. Lily probably wasn't heavier than two pounds.

I heard the screaming, and it is a fact that the children aren't likely to ever scream unless a death is imminent. I was already in my pajamas and a robe, but I didn't wait to dress but got out fast with Gwen following.

In an instant I saw what had happened. There was Buck with Lily between his jaws parading back and forth on the lawn, tail throbbing with pride. When the children saw me they stopped chasing him. I took a few steps in his direction and then gave a low whistle. Buck turned. His ears, floppy as they were, seemed to perk up. He was doing precisely as he had been bred to do. He was doing it well. It was for him a proud moment.

So he came to me then, tail throbbing, the eyes shining and he sat in front of me. I put out my hand. He dropped the duck into it. I praised him, patted him on the head, and then the children had him by the collar and were leading him back to the kennel where the other two dogs were riotous with jealousy.

For Lily it was lucky it had been Buck. Either of the other two, Brig or Eekim, might have crushed the life from her. But Buck was soft-mouthed, so soft-mouthed, in fact, that when he was learning to retrieve, his quarry often slipped from his grasp and went free.

In time he learned to hold fast, at least so any furred or feathered thing might not slip away, but still so gently that only rarely did his long, white teeth ever break skin.

Lily was in a lather, of course, but otherwise she was all right.

"Put her in a cage," I said, "at least for tonight."

(19

Friday turned out to be an Indian summer day. There were silver spider threads hanging on the breeze, and a dandelion, which had hidden beneath leaves to escape the frost, put up a face of gold.

The night before Lily's fate had been decided. She would go to the ponds, and if she didn't make it among the society of ducks, there would always be a chance she'd come back up the hill looking for help.

"You want to see her go?" I asked Gwen.

"In a minute."

So while I waited in the sun-room, the girls went out where they'd caged Lily in the pet compound and brought her in.

The duck looked no worse for her terrifying experience with the dog, so we all walked down across the lawn, between Fish Pond and Blue Pool, until we were standing among the small spruce on the edge of Mill Pond.

Out in front of us there was a scattering of ducks. Pete was among them, and when the flock saw us, they dipped their heads, quacked softly, and swam in quick circles.

I lifted Lily, held her high for perhaps ten seconds so she could survey her surroundings, and then tossed her into the air. She flew well for a few hundred feet and then slanted down and planed along the water. For a moment she only floated there. Then she dipped, and in an ecstasy of bobbing, showered water pearls down her graceful neck, back over her brown feathers.

All the other ducks except Pete ignored her. He swam slowly over, bobbing a welcome with his emerald head, and then in front of her flapped his wings so the water flew. At first she sat still with her neck pulled in, her head tucked tight. Then when Pete swam along side dipping and stretching in a play at courtship, she seemed to relax. Pete backed off and swam around her a half-dozen times as though looking her over, and then started off for the cattails with her in tow.

While we watched them, they disappeared, and we all turned, and without a word, went back up to the house.

I made a half-dozen false starts then on a column I wanted to write, but finally gave it up and went to the sun room to watch the sun set. While I was there the children came in.

"They're together," Dianne said.

"You mean Pete and Lily?"

"Yes," Mary said, "they're staying together."

The children went out then to finish their chores, and I picked up one of the two pairs of binoculars from the ledge by my chair. I quickly found the duck flock and then spotted the little brown hen and the green-headed drake side-by-side, separated a little from the others.

"Gwen," I called, "come and take a look."

"It's wonderful," she said, putting the glasses down.

The sun was gone now, but the colors were still in the sky and their reflection was still in the water where the ducks floated.

I lighted my pipe, and Gwen brought me coffee. As I puffed between sips of coffee, Gwen took a chair across the room from me.

"You know what tomorrow is?" she asked.

"Sure, tomorrow is Saturday."

"I don't mean that."

"Then what do you mean?"

"Tomorrow the duck hunting season opens."

I looked toward the rack in the corner which held my many hunting guns.

"You going to go?" she asked.

"I don't have a license."

"You could get one. The Sport Shack in Muskego is open until nine."

I blew out a cloud of smoke. In the dim light it hung like blue gauze on the still air.

"You've come to think hunting is barbaric, haven't you?" She made it sound almost like an accusation.

"Not really," I said.

"But you do. I can tell. You think it isn't civilized."

"Maybe," I hedged.

"But you used to love it so!"

"In ways I still do," I admitted.

"Then why don't you just go? It might relax you. You've been working so hard again."

I only shrugged.

"Is it because you think it's barbaric?"

"Barbarism is an honest emotion," I said. "We come by it naturally. Among other things, it means to 'do things in a wild way.' We were barbarians for countless thousands of years."

"But now you think it's time to change?" It was a question.

"I don't know. I really mean that, I *don't* know," I said, "but anyway, I think maybe I'll just skip it tomorrow. Maybe skip it for this year."

"I sort of thought you might."

She got up and started toward the kitchen. In front of the gun rack she stopped. "Your guns are getting dusty," she said.

"I know," I nodded. "They need oil, too. Tomorrow. Maybe tomorrow I'll take care of them."

Epilogue

Mr. Wallace Exman, Senior Editor
Holt, Rinehart and Winston, Inc.

Dear Wally:

As the manuscript leaves me for the last time, be advised that Pete is alive and doing well.

It was just six years ago that I amputated his leg, so by now he must be seven, maybe eight, years old.

I regret that I never realized that I might someday write about him, other than casually. Then I would have taken pictures each season with which to illustrate this book. But, of course, that was one of the things furthest from my mind.

This fall there is only one child, Mary, left at Little Lakes. Still the others—Sharon, SuZanne, Deborah, and Dianne—go down to the ponds to see Pete when they visit.

Anyway, we're hoping he's got more years, because Little Lakes won't be quite the same without him.

Cordially,

Mel Ellis

P.S. I did go hunting. But only two times.